ALL THINGS CONSIDERED...

Trials, Tribulations, Temptations and Triumphs
of Being Christian in Modern-Day America

Kenneth L. Wilson

Christian Herald Books
Chappaqua, New York

*To my loving wife Juanita, who has
put up with me for 35 years (so far),
and to our two daughters and two sons
who I hope may remember us for more
than our words.*

Contents

I. Looking Within

II. Looking Around

III. Looking Up

ALL THINGS CONSIDERED...

Foreword

All Things Considered takes its name from a regular feature in *Christian Herald* magazine which I have written for ten years. *Have Faith Without Fear* was the first book to result, and this is the second. Of course, *All Things Considered* doesn't consider all things, just many things, most of them things that do not seem to me to get adequate consideration and some of them very little, indeed. We so readily see in the gospel what we expect to see or want to see or our culture allows us to see. Rather than look at the Scriptures, it is my purpose to let the Scriptures look at me and at us and at the world in which we live.

These pieces do not intend to say "all" that can be said and that perhaps ought to be said about whatever "thing" it is. Adding to what has been said already by others, I hope they may round out truth by at least a small sliver here and there. If nothing else, they may motivate you in either agreement or disagreement to think of something I have not thought of. As is life itself, this book is made up of a miscellany of thoughts, not all of them logically following each other, some of them probably seeming to contradict others, none of them offering "the last word."

God's love is wide and deep—and available. That's the important word to be said.

Kenneth L. Wilson

ALL THINGS CONSIDERED...

I. Looking Within

It Doesn't Say,
Ye Are The Pepper of the Earth

I ONCE HAD A COUSIN who put pepper on ice cream, but I think she was just hoping to get attention. When I tried it, it didn't do anything for me. It doesn't take as much pepper to do whatever normal people do with it, as it takes salt, for example. Even the comparative size or number of holes in the salt and pepper shakers tells you that much. Someone, generations of shakermakers back, recognized that we need more salt than pepper in life. Jesus did not say, "Ye are the pepper of the earth," but there are those of his followers who never quite got the right message.

One could, of course, speak of the "peppery" nature of some of the brethren. Even the dictionary makes it a personality trait: "having a hot temper, touchy." In addition are such afterthoughts as "hot, pungent, fiery, stinging." All of which means that if you're peppery, you're ready to leap to the barricades and earnestly contend at a moment's notice. Now, maybe it's nice, for balance, to have that quality in a few people, or to have a little of it in any of us, but a little goes a long way. That's why pepper holes are smaller than salt holes; you like to know the pepper is there, if you ever have to get at it, but you don't want it all over everything.

But, there must be other reasons why Jesus said we are

15

or ought to be the salt of the earth and not the pepper of the earth. (And not, come to think of it, the sugar of the earth, but that's another story.) Salt, for one thing, is a preservative. This is not exactly news, but what may be news is that it means there is something worth preserving where we are, besides us. Preservatives keep things from spoiling, from going bad. If we are salt, that is one of our jobs. If this is the case, we are never elated when something or someone goes bad, for the going bad reflects upon the preservative—us. ("Salt is never glad when others go wrong," I Cor. 13:6, Moffatt and Wilson.)

Pepper calls attention to itself. That is its business. Salt, on the other hand (unless it is overdone), calls attention to what it salts. Salt in the proper measure on the potatoes sends out a message that, being interpreted, reads, "Hey, these potatoes are good!" Pepper, whatever you put it on, calls attention to itself. That is what it is supposed to do. It's a little like the sauce on spaghetti. Who eats spaghetti for the tongue-tingling taste of unadorned spaghetti? If someone says, "This is great spaghetti!" you may be sure he is talking about something other than spaghetti. He is talking about what's on it. That's the way pepper, too, works. It shouts, "Hey, that's me you taste!"

And so I think that Jesus didn't say, "You are the pepper of the earth," because he didn't expect us to call attention to ourselves but to make something or someone else palatable, acceptable, zestful. If he had said pepper, it wouldn't take that much pepper. But salt—it takes a lot of salt.

The peppery, here-I-am-and-don't-you-forget-it Christian goes a long way. Just a comparative smidgeon takes care of demands. But there is always a need for the it's-my-job-to-make-you-look-better Christian. There is always an opening for the Christian who is willing to push the other person forward, bear him up, keep him at his best, let him be paid the compliment, preserve his goings out and comings in.

16

Did You See That?
He Hit My <u>Other</u> Cheek!

BECAUSE we live in a technological age, we seem to believe that there is a technology for being Christian, and that all we have to do is push the right buttons and use the right motivating words. If a sales pitch for a cabbage slicer can be refined to the point where it racks up customers, why can't evangelization techniques be perfected that will bring prospects clamoring to the church door? When one effective believer comes up with something that "works," everyone wants to try it. We Christians chase each other in circles, trying to find our answers in someone else's technique.

What the books and the courses and the teachers and the exhorters do not say is that a particular technique worked at a particular time in a particular place, not because it was a successful technique but because it was the lifestyle and the heartbeat and the passion of someone who probably did not know anything about technique.

Some people spend time analyzing the technique of Jesus. I don't think he had any. He was simply being himself, caring about men and women who were locked into all kinds of imprisoning ideas and circumstances. When I hear people talking about what a great psychologist or great teacher or even great preacher Jesus was, I think they have missed the point. He may have been all these, but only without knowing, or perhaps caring, that he was any of them. We do not achieve Christlikeness by discovering his techniques and using them. We achieve it by letting him live through us, through our own lifestyle, our own techniques. We achieve it by caring about people in his name, genuinely caring, without an instruction book in one hand (even if it happens to be the Bible), while we pick up the cup of cold water with the other. There is a

17

certain intuitiveness that makes the Christian life what it is, a certain impulsive compassion, a dynamic presence of the Holy Spirit, if you will. Knowing the rules does not necessarily make a Christian more loving. But when he is loving, he has some sixth sense about the rules.

There are, in fact, happenings that may never work as techniques. Because we have seldom considered that this is so, we feel let down when we have been self-consciously Christian in some incident or other and it hasn't paid off in success. We have supposed that having been struck on one cheek, if we turn the other we will so embarrass, so overwhelm, so spiritually shatter the striker that we will achieve instant reconciliation. Instead, he may let us have it on the other cheek, too. Not always. But enough of the time so that we can never be sure. The point is, you don't do it for what perhaps will happen in your opponent's soul, but for what will assuredly happen in yours. "Turning the other cheek" helps you blot out your bitterness, for now you are voluntarily vulnerable. Watching out of the corner of your eye to see what impression you're making on the other person almost insures that it won't work. At least, it insures that it won't do anything useful for your own bitterness.

By the immediacy with which such things are measured, it sometimes pays to be dishonest. Whether, and how much, honesty pays is not the Christian's measure. Tithing as a purse-fattening technique is something less than Christian stewardship, purse-fattening or not. Joy is never a payoff for calculated conduct. Joy comes from a consecrated recklessness of spirit, a bubbling up of deep springs that have no faucet either for turning on or turning off.

Forget It!

THERE IS a lot of remembering that needs to be done these days, but I have a feeling that often the wrong people are doing it. The same applies to forgetting.

Here's the way it goes. Someone gives a gift, and when

the recipient begins offering his thanks, the giver becomes, or thinks he's supposed to become, embarrassed, and says, "Forget it!" Actually, it is not the recipient, who, for his own strength of character, can or ought to forget it, but the giver. Yet, etiquette being what it is, were the receiver to say to the giver, "Forget it!" there would be a great to-do and all sorts of charges of ungratefulness.

The one receiving the gift, therefore, can't offer the giver an important and neglected piece of advice, and so I would like to do it for him: "Forget it!" I'd like to say it to myself when I play the pleasurable role of giver, and to the whole Christian establishment, and to the whole American establishment. For as anybody can see who is not blinded by power politics either personal, ecclesiastical or national, we are not above using our gifts to buy, or to try to buy, love, loyalty, friendship, even faith. We don't really believe the words in the hymn "I Would Be True" that we so glibly sing: "I would be giving and forget the gift." When it comes to recalling what we have ever done for anyone, we have memories like elephants.

"I've worked my fingers to the bone for you," a parent has been known to say to the child, meaning that the child is indentured in perpetuity by parental sacrifice. Although parental sacrifice is something the child should remember, it is something the parent should forget, for reasons of mental health, if nothing else.

I have seen sacks of famine relief food stamped large with the words, "This food is a gift from the citizens of the United States of America." Perhaps some of that is necessary, the state of international credit-grabbing being what it is. But horn-blowing philanthropy gives rise to the national givers' lament, "After all we did for them, look how they're voting in the U.N."

The church has been as guilty of this sort of thing as anyone. We Christians have a very long, very commercial memory when we contemplate what we have poured into a country and then "lost" by a change of government or religious mood. Which means that we were selling Christianity on the installment plan, not doing what we did because we cared about the people themselves. It would be nice if those who received the gifts would remember—and I have the feeling that deep down, many of them do, or would if we didn't keep telling them they should—but we dare not be the ones to remind them. The church has not always listened to its own hymn. We've cherished those merit badges!

Years ago, missionary Lillian Dickson of Taiwan told me, "You can do anything you want to do, if you don't care who gets the credit for it." Could it be that so much of the time in so much that we do, the bookkeeping is more important than the doing? If that is true, our giving is sham, and we ought to call it by a more honest name. The real test for my giving, for America's giving, for the church's giving, is whether we are willing to leave off the return address on the label. It would take superior brands of unselfish caring, of Americanism, yes, of Christian commitment, to give generously and compassionately and then tell ourselves, "Forget it!"

Honk, If You Love Jesus

SO HELP ME, that's what I read on the bumper sticker on the car ahead. I didn't honk. Mainly, perhaps, because I don't like to be turned on and off like a light switch. I have been in certain church services when the minister shouted, "Everybody say 'Amen! '" and I didn't say Amen, either. There are some things that lose meaning very easily, at least for me. Like the ice cream freezer I saw in a store recently. It was the kind in a wooden tub, but was, incredibly, powered by an electric motor. It is my conviction that if you don't crank an ice cream freezer by hand, you shouldn't be making ice cream in a freezer in the first place. For it's not that homemade freezer ice cream is so great, but that the fun of making it is so great. Take away the cranking and what have you got? There are some things you cannot automate or mass produce or even program, and have anything left worth having.

It isn't as if I would not be very happy to encounter even an occasional motorist who loves Jesus. But I would like to see the loving proved by something more than a honk. The other morning when I momentarily blocked a lady driver's path, *she* honked. I promptly received the impression that she did not love me and I doubt if she loved Jesus, for the look she flashed my way was one of instant anger. For all I know, she was a very sane and a very nice person and maybe even a Christian when she didn't have a hundred-and-some horsepower at her disposal.

All of which indicates that what I would most value on the highway from one who loves Jesus is not a honk either of rebuke or of testimony, but a Christian style of driving. But I suppose no one would buy a bumper sticker that reads, "Drive courteously, if you love Jesus." It's easier to honk. That's the story of my life as a Christian, I am afraid, and possibly of yours. It's easier to make a noise than progress. It's easier to talk about being loving than it is to be loving (or even than to be lovable). Honking, for the average church member, is what it's all about. How wrong can we get?

Take "witnessing," for example. I am sure that once in a while someone emphasizes that witnessing is not all talk, but from what I have seen and heard, it must be only once in a while. When the witnessing is out of the way—sort of like the day's Good Turn—one normally goes about one's pursuits in a manner as shrewd or calculating or cussed as the job calls for. Real witnessing, in the dusty Galilean road sense, is the essence of life itself. It's not a matter of a honk here and a honk there, but of one's total lifestyle, wherever and whenever.

A neglected word in religious circles is "winsome." That doesn't mean making eyes or showing dimples or slapping backs, but being the kind of person who by sheer being and presence raises the sights and capabilities of those whose lives he touches. It's the quality of life that makes clear one is aware of others and their well-being, even if one happens to be behind the wheel of a car—the spot these days to take a difficult test of Christian love.

There's just no substitute for what Jesus called taking up your cross and following him. Certainly a honk is no substitute. There is no easy out for commitment. But then the man or woman who is genuinely committed is not looking for one.

You Can Always <u>Be</u> an Answer

I DO NOT RECALL at what airport our plane had just landed, nor when. As we slowed to a stop, a small pickup truck darted in front of us. When the back of the truck swung around into the line of view of those of us on the plane, I saw a large sign fastened to the tailgate. In big black letters on a bright yellow background were the words, FOLLOW ME.

The sign didn't say, LISTEN TO ME. It didn't say, I'LL TELL YOU WHERE TO GO. It said, FOLLOW ME. That means, GO WHERE I GO, DO WHAT I DO. And our plane did just that, and presently we were pulling up to our gate.

It would seem to be an audacious statement, if it were a sign carried by those who call themselves Christians. It would seem to promise more than we can deliver. In fact, some of us do not react well to those who claim to have all the answers and know all the ways, or who, indeed, insist there *are* discernible answers to all the questions that may be asked. But I think that in such cases our resentment is directed at those who are *giving* answers and not at those who are *being* answers.

You may not always be able to give an answer. But where you are, in your own way, with your own talents, with the measure of faith God has given you, you can always *be* some kind of answer.

How did we ever get so far from the biblical concept of basic witnessing? How did we get all that way from being to saying? Why is it that when we try to measure orthodoxy, we almost always do it in words, and almost never in actions?

Well, for one thing, it's easier to say what someone else should do than it is to be what someone else should be. Sometimes at *Christian Herald* we receive a manuscript from a writer who notes, "The Holy Spirit told me to send this to you." Sometimes the Holy Spirit tells us to return it, and we do this as gently as possible. The Holy Spirit has to speak for himself, and in a manuscript, he does it through what is there, and in our lives, through what is there.

Did you ever stop to think of how few direct answers Jesus ever gave to questions put to him? For example, there was the time John the Baptist sent members of his team to check out the Master's credentials. "Art thou he that should come?" they asked, implying, "All you have to do is say so and we'll carry back the good word." I think there would have been something demeaningly defensive about Jesus' having to say, "Absolutely, I'm the one! You have my word on it." Furthermore, can the real question be answered in those terms?

Instead, he said, "Tell John what you have seen. That the blind see, the lame walk, the sick are healed, the deaf hear, the dead are raised, the poor have the gospel preached to them."

When John's men check us out and ask, "Are you his disciple?" how do we respond? Can we say, "Look at what's happening, and judge for yourself"? Look at my home. Look at me on the job. Look at where I put my priorities. Look at what I think is important. Is there healing where I am? Does someone hurt less or hurt more because I am there? Am I a peacemaker or a conflict bringer? Do I get my kicks out of downgrading someone or out of upgrading him? Is someone closer to God because I have passed by?

Or would we have to admit, "Well, actually, there's not much to see—but we sure believe a lot!" For the one looking at us, it could well be that seeing is believing.

How Am I Punctuating My Faith?

TODAY, STUDENTS, let's open our books to the section on punctuation marks. You will notice immediately that there are many punctuation marks, including colons, semicolons, hyphens, apostrophes and other odds and ends. They all have certain jobs to do, but we will direct our attention to the subsection which deals with the punctuation marks that go at the end of a sentence.

There are three of these, of which the simplest is the period. This (.) is a period. It takes very little effort to make one. I mean, even if you can't write anything else, you can write a period. No matter whether your penmanship is good or poor, your period will look as good as anybody else's. Handwriting experts can do very little with periods, when it comes to analyzing the character of the writer, except when somebody makes his periods look like small x's, and it is my private opinion that these are not really periods at all. All a period was ever intended to be was small and round and black (or blue or some other color, as the case may be).

If you have three periods written one after another (. . .), or four if at the end of a sentence (. . . .), this does not, contrary to logic, emphasize that this is indeed, indisputedly, unequivocally, the end. It means, rather, that it isn't, because something has been left out. There is a word for this, but it is hard to spell.

The job of the period is to mark the end of what is called a declarative sentence, which is a sentence you simply declare, drop on somebody's doorstep, so to speak, and they either like it or lump it. There it is. Notice how authoritative, how aggressive, the period looks in that last sentence. It takes a lot of courage to argue with a period. They are tough little cookies. In England, a period is called a "full stop," which is a good name for it.

So much for the period. Fix carefully in your mind what one looks like and you'll never forget it.

The second of the three major punctuating indicators is

the interrogation point, more popularly known as the question mark. It looks like (?) this. Like the other major indicators, this comes at the end of the sentence, which sometimes is too late to be of any help. You may be reading a sentence with a great deal of assurance, and then at the very end come to a ? and all your security goes down the drain. If you had just had a little more time to get used to the idea, there would have been no trouble at all. The Spanish speaking (and writing) peoples of the world are miles ahead of us on this, for they give fair warning at the beginning of the sentence that it's going to turn out to be a question. They do this by printing an upside-down question mark before the first word. As to why it is upside-down, you'll have to ask a Spaniard. (There is, it should be noted, a rightside-up one at the conclusion of their sentence also, which may make you feel better.)

IN a spoken sentence, the only way anybody has of knowing that a question mark is there is the rising inflection at the finish. Sometimes—if you're reading aloud—the question mark looms up before you can get your inflection turned in the proper direction. The Spanish method would help in this regard, too; you would have the whole sentence in which to build up to a finale, and if you didn't have your inflection in hand by then, it would be your own fault. This still doesn't take care of conversational, made-up-on-the-spot sentences, which one suspects are sometimes designed to come out halfway between a flat statement and a defensive question. (There is no punctuation mark for *that*.)

To use a question mark means confessing that there is something you don't know. That's why some people do not like them. A question mark (?) even looks like a question mark, especially the top half, which is more than you can say for a semicolon, neither half of which looks like anything very original. Notice the sinuous sweep of a question mark, the voluptuous curves. Believe me, they aren't there for nothing!

Try making one for yourself. Take the period, which you have previously written, and put the hook on top and you've got a question mark. (How Spaniards draw their upside-down ones, you may discover by watching a Spanish bill collector writing a letter.)

So we come to the last of the trio of major punctuation marks. You are correct, it is the exclamation (!) point. Although possessing the same handicap of positioning as the question mark, the exclamation point makes you glad you saw the thing through, when you get there. If a period is placid, and a question mark is doubtful, an exclamation point is excited. Its job is to convey excitement, communicate it, make other people excited.

Now, when some individuals discover the exclamation point, they go wild. They write, speak and live in exclamation points, which gets a little tiring. When every sentence is punctuated with excitement, you soon don't get excited about anything. There is a church in Pittsburgh, whose major deviation from conservatism is not theological but punctuational. In this church's bulletin, every notice is in capitals followed by not one but four exclamation points ! ! ! ! ! (The last one here is my own.) With equal degrees of excitement, the preparer of the bulletin calls attention to THE END OF THE WORLD! ! ! ! and POT LUCK SUPPER! ! ! ! All of which proves that an exclamation point does not necessarily enthusiasm make, nor four of them an emotional crisis. There was, after all, the boy who cried "Wolf!" and as you can see, he cried it with an exclamation point.

WHICH brings us to the observation that if you took away the exclamation point from some utterances (even "Wolf") you wouldn't have much left. Try stripping it from Merry Christmas, for example. Without an exclamation point, it just lies there. Or Happy New Year or Happy Birthday. Neither of them looks happy at all. They're just sort of waiting for something to occur. A question mark wouldn't do them any good, either. HAPPY NEW YEAR?

With that sort of punctuation, you feel terrible, just seeing it in print. All the hope and excitement is gone, and you're left holding a bag of uncertainties.

It has taken me a long time to get around to saying what I'm trying to say—that Christians are, by all they do and the way they do it, punctuating their lifestyles for better or for worse. There is a time and place for dogmatic, self-assured periods in our faith. The period is the basic punctuation mark for any way of life. You've *got* to have something to go on, something to build on. Periods are the building blocks. A period affirms. It says quietly, "I believe." It says without fanfare, "For me, this is the way it is." You've got to start with something, and the something is an affirmation.

BUT for many of us, that's it, period. Faith, we need to remember, goes and grows with questions. Somewhere, sometime, even inadvertently, we will wind up with a question mark that somebody has sneaked in at the end of one of our favorite beliefs. It doesn't have to upset or dismay us if we admit ahead of time that this is the way life is. There *will be* question marks. And some of them ought to be our own. Some of them will be those of our children. Some of them may be hard ones for us and hard ones for them, but the pains are growing pains. Yet questions only, as a total way of life, produce cynicism, bitterness, sourness. How to keep the affirmations and the doubts in proper balance, that is the skill we must always be learning but which we shall never completely master.

And the exclamation points! What seasoning they give to faith and life. Faith is affirming. It is questioning. It is celebration, too, and this is so easy to neglect. What a grace it is to be enthusiastic, daring, adventuresome, excited, alive. And how much more whole, how much more real, how much more alive we can be if we punctuate our lifestyle properly.

Alive. Just barely.

Alive? Surely we can do better than that.

Alive! That's what a Christian was meant to be!

Don't You Hear the Bells Now Ringing? Frankly, No

ONE of the unfortunate side effects of personal testimony is the implication that exactly what happened to you should and can happen to everyone else or even to someone else. Having achieved, we want to lock others into the same level of achievement. Christian freedom, to stay alive, repeatedly has to burst through someone else's bars.

There are causes, arguments, ideas to which I immediately respond. They strike a chord in me. There are others that leave me quite untwanged, however worthy they may be. I can either feel guilty that I don't vibrate as someone else does, or I can admit that I just may be on a different wavelength. My own nature, heritage, talents and opportunities urge me in one direction while those of another person urge him in a different direction. Must I go with him, or he with me, just to keep up a united front?

This is one of the assumptions that has often bothered me in church. Someone gets what he thinks is a big idea and launches a "let us do this" (or, more often, a "let's *you* do this") campaign. Out of a duty reflex, everyone pitches in, hating every minute of it. Now, there are things that have to be done corporately or not at all. And not everyone will equally enjoy the doing for they are not all fun things. But there are other experiences and tasks which not only cannot be achieved or performed corporately but which cannot be duplicated privately. And yet, in church, duplication is so often the name of the game and the Christian tends to see evangelism as a kind of spiritual Xerox machine, turning out precise copies of himself.

"Don't you hear the bells now ringing? Don't you hear the angels singing?" The chances are good that I don't—not when and how someone thinks I should. I've quit feeling bad about that because, for one thing, it evens out. For another, a Christian experience to be authentic need not parallel mine nor mine someone else's.

Some Christians are contemplative in their faith—thank God for them. They glory in the mystery and mystique. Others prefer to show their faith through community—thank God for them. I must confess that, to me, worship is not an end in itself. I do not think of it as something that stands alone, is self-contained, can be looked at, is something I come specifically to do. Rather, I see it as a by-product. But not everyone feels that way and together we have a better chance of approximating the whole truth than separately.

Name whatever it is that religiously turns you on, whether building a low-cost housing project or speaking in tongues, and the same thing applies. To say that because I think the Bible says a certain thing, you have to think so, too, is to say that we will forever be squeezing souls out of shape in order to get them into somebody else's shoes.

Church music (or any kind of music, for that matter) is an area where there is, to put it mildly, a lack of unanimity. I think that "educating" people to good church music is a lost cause, mainly because it is not that clear what is good and why it is good. I gag at some of the schmaltzy (yes, and sexy) gospel music which could as well be waltzed to as prayed by. Those angels just aren't singing for me. But they must be singing for somebody, judging by their state of health. Fine! Just so other Christians keep their cotton-picking hands off *my* angels.

I Am the Light of the World?

YOU TEND to get very few takers, when the cool statement from the Sermon on the Mount turns into a hot question. For when you stop to think about it, you know that in the process of giving light, something or someone has to be used up, and you don't propose for it to be you. It may be that in a laboratory it is possible to produce totally cold light, but any light that I have had anything to do with burns up, is consumed in the very act of being light, whether the kerosene and wick in a lantern or the filament in an electric bulb. Man's proverbial striving is for more light and less heat, but so far, at least, we can't have light without heat. "Cool it, man!" in our state of technology and ideology may be simply another way of saying, "Put out the light."

So anybody who is serious about accepting the assignment of being the light of the world had better know that it's going to take something out of him. It will cost. But, then, mere existence costs. Burning, they tell me, is oxidation, chemically speaking. But so is rusting, rotting, corroding—these are slow-motion forms of burning. Decay is, in other words, light that didn't make it. Therefore, if your foremost interest is a place to hide, there isn't any. And as for me, I would rather try, with some effort, to be the light of the world than, without any effort, to be the rust of the world.

But I admit that it would all sound so much more attainable if it weren't quite so ambitious. *The* light of the world. Not *a* light of the world. Little old me, *the* light of the world? Heaven help the world! Yet . . . yet . . . how do you separate light into pieces or pools or puddles? Light, however big or small, wherever, whenever, is the dispelling of darkness, the revealing of what is waiting to be seen. Light is light, whether match-size or Kleig-size. Any ray of light is *the* light. There are indeed Christians and religious bodies who like to think that they personally, exclusively, totally, have the light. But light is not something you have. It is something you are. It is not a commodity you pridefully manage to corner. It is a humble willingness to give yourself.

When you get right down to it, how small is small and how big is big, lightwise? I enjoy visiting lighthouses along the coast. I am always amazed that it is possible to get such a brilliant beam out of such a very small source of light. It's not for nothing that we measure light in candlepower! The light seen by mariners is done pretty much with mirrors. The small light in the lighthouse, placed in front of mirrors and behind magnifying lenses, becomes a big light. Is it so far wrong to say that the Sermon on the Mount kind of light is also done with mirrors? Commitment, concern, a compassionate sense of timing magnify and mirror the candlepower of anyone willing to give himself to being even a small light. Sometimes, and I suspect most of the time, the mirrors and lenses are beyond our conscious control. God is in charge of that department. Some of the most faithful lights never seemed at the time to shine very far. It is perhaps enough if they—we—light even a few steps of someone's way.

Anybody here willing to be the light? The normal response is an incredulous, "You mean *me?*" But faith, which alone satisfies our terrible longing for meaning and motivation, reads it happily and confidently. "You mean me!"

All Spiritual Business Is Local

SOME YEARS AGO the American Newspaper Publishers Association ran a campaign to encourage advertising in newspapers. The theme: "All Business Is Local." The point was that however national or international an advertising effort, the ultimate sale is made to the individual buyer where he lives or works. You may hear and see the advantages of a particular car on a nationwide telecast or read about it in a nationally circulated magazine or be impressed with it on an out-of-state trip, but the sale is culminated at your friendly local car dealer's showroom. You could become convinced that you can't live without a certain breakfast food or dog biscuit, go around unconsciously humming the jingles that promote them, but to buy the product you go to your neighborhood grocery or supermarket. Goods sold by mail require a local point of response—the mailbox into which you drop your order.

You may believe that something is absolutely the greatest, but if you don't authenticate your conviction with some kind of transaction, no business is being done, and the place where the authentication takes place and has to take place is where you live. You could write to the network and tell them how much you like the product, how clever the advertising is, how your little boy goes around singing, "Oh, what a relief it is!" and it might make the company feel good and might even make you feel good, but it's not business. Business comes, in that case, at the drugstore counter. Business happens only when there is a response.

It seems to me the newspaper publishers were stretching it a little when they attempted to tie this fact of life solely to newspaper advertising. Aside from that, it is a fact of life to be reckoned with. And it is a fact also of spiritual life. All spiritual business is local, a point that Jesus, Paul, James and others made repeatedly.

There is no general way of living as a Christian—there are only specific ways. The Christian faith is not some vague, formless, roseate glow one cultivates, but a belief, a commitment that becomes operative in what one does. One can go around singing the "jingles," the hymns and gospel songs, and they may encourage commitment or be some indication that there has been one, but until a transaction has taken place, there is no "business." One may have the creedal selling points down pat, as one may know which word is coming next in an often-heard television or radio commercial, but what the advertiser is really interested in is not your familiarity with the commercial but your use of the product.

More and more of our religion seems to be general and less and less of it local. We in the church have rightly become conscious of global needs. But seeing the needs, hearing about them, feeling bad about them is different from doing something about them. We think we're doing a lot of spiritual business just by talking, discussing, but the real business takes place when an individual puts a piece of his life, his resources, on the line. The rich young ruler who came to Jesus knew all the commercials and jingles. His faith was ideologically flawless. But it wasn't local. He was not of the world, but neither was he in it.

We need often to be reminded that the church itself is local. One may belong to the Church Universal, but it's not where you conduct business. At the local level, *the* Church becomes *a* church. That's where it happens. That's where the global becomes specific—sometimes uncomfortably so.

Don't Look at Me – Judas Is the One Over There

IT IS ALWAYS the one who is most faithful who wonders if he is faithful enough, the one who loves most deeply who doubts that he loves enough, the one who is most compassionate who questions that he is caring enough, the one who is most sacrificial who worries that he has not given enough.

That is why, to me Judas plays only a small part in the story of Judas. When Jesus says to his disciples, "One of you shall betray me," the story is not that Judas knows he is Judas but that eleven other supposedly totally committed disciples think they might be. "They began every one of them to say unto him, Lord, is it I?"

What, I wonder did each of them see within himself that caused him to think he might be the one? Take John, for example, especially loved by Jesus. Was he murmuring merely a polite comment when he said, "Lord, is it I?"— the way we say, "How are you?" and do not wait for an answer? Or did he know something about himself that we don't know, just as we know something about ourselves that we do not discuss with others and that we hide even from our own thoughts?

Crisis moments are revealing. They strip away carefully cultivated responses and force us to see ourselves for what we are. It is in the impulsive, unpremeditated response that we are most fully revealed. We have intended that we would do or never do this or that, then suddenly the moment is upon us, there is no time to rehearse and out of all we are and have ever been, we react. That is why it is impossibly smug for us to judge another person's action by what we think we would have done in the situation, had we been there. We can never wholly divorce ourselves from personal or national betrayal, for we, too, harbor seeds of betrayal. We can only shake our heads sorrowfully, ponder, "Lord, is it I?" and never be entirely sure that it is not.

Matthew wondered if he did not qualify as a betrayer. Matthew was experienced in such things. A former tax collector, he had lived by wits, avarice and ambition. Surely he had betrayed, which is to say he had spoken up or remained silent for personal advantage or convenience. He knew how it was done. Something lurking in a dark corner of his soul gave him reason to ask, "Is it I?" Peter couldn't visualize himself as denying his Master, but he must have thought he was capable of betrayal, for he asked, "Lord, is it I?"

Around the table they went. "Every one of them." Even Judas. Was he already sure? Or did he think that he was simply speeding up the coming of the Kingdom, prodding Jesus to make it all happen right now? That would explain his later suicide—remorse at discovering the Kingdom cannot come by coup. I wonder if his sin was that he was so evil or simply that he was so practical? His was the Gospel According to Judas, and his gospel has had its own followers and sometimes we have been they.

"Lord, is it I?" What did they all see when they suddenly had to look deep into their souls? What do I see when I look deep into mine? And what do we miss seeing when we self-righteously turn the question from ourselves to other betrayers, past or present?

Receiving — the Other Half of Giving

PAUL SAYS in the Book of Acts, "It is more blessed to give than to receive," and he is verily not kidding. Receiving, contrary to popular expectation, is sometimes not blessed at all. In fact, receiving may not only be no fun, but may bring one about as close to total humiliation as it is possible to come.

More blessed to give than to receive? You just bet it is! Giving provides uncounted kicks in satisfaction, ego-boosting, more-than-thou-ness, great-white-fathering, lady-of-the-manorism. Much of this is the fault of the giver and of those who promote giving, extracting every pound of fleshly delight from it. The gift without the giver is bare. But the gift *with* the giver—eternally, condescendingly, suspiciously with—is not bare enough. Arrogant giving can turn the best of gifts to ashes.

But so can graceless receiving.

While it is quite true that givers, even Christian givers, can refine and Christianize their motivations and methods, I would not wish to discourage anyone from giving, even if clumsily. It is too easy to take refuge in the excuse that because one does not know how to give gracefully, one will therefore not give at all. Keep those cards and letters and gifts coming, folks—for whatever reason—and those at the receiving end will do their best to redeem them.

For at least a part of the problem has been with the receiver. Let him who would learn how to give, first learn how to receive. Gracious receiving is simply not one of the most-practiced arts of our time. Since childhood, we have been taught to give, from kindergarten and the primary department up. "Billy, share your toys with Bobby," the teacher says, and finally achieves the victory of seeing Billy reluctantly hand over a toy to Bobby—who takes it as his right or who is still mad about the whole thing or who will have nothing to do with it. Bobby has been on the short end. Nobody has taught us Bobbies how to receive.

Oh, they drill into us the importance of saying thank-you. But as far as I can recall, no one ever tried to teach me the importance of *feeling* thank-you. It was always something I was to say, not something I was to experience. And because it was primarily for saying, it was primarily for the benefit of the giver, not of the getter.

We by our overbalanced emphasis upon giving, in church and out, have made receiving into something sub-standard, second-rate, disreputable, almost dirty. Yet, receiving, too, can be a creative force. Receiving requires its own graces, and they do not come easily, considering our present social and institutional pressures. They must be learned, even as the graces of giving must be learned. And then—and this is the part we so seldom realize—once learned, the techniques must be forgotten in the doing, else they become merely a practicing of scales and not a spontaneous, free-flowing lifestyle.

But the how necessarily comes first. How do you go about becoming a gracious receiver—and why? Well, first of all, we have to do so much more receiving than giving. That's simply the way life is. So much comes to each of us that we shall never be able to repay in coin or in kind. Life itself is one of those blessings. The world itself is another. Beauty itself. Some things are just there, as God is there. We had no part in their being there. They are a found dollar on the sidewalk. What do you do with it? Hope that the one who lost it will come back, and so let it lie? Pick it up, but feel guilty ever after that you were the one who found it? Try to discover the owner, which may be an all but impossible task?

THE analogy is obviously not perfect, for it is all too easy to rationalize anything to our own advantage. Yet, here we are with so much for which we have had so little responsi-bility. Without any effort on our part, we came along in the "right" century, in the "right" country, in the "right"

36

family—as every happy man anywhere in the world from the beginning of time must have felt. And at this season of the year when we try to bring our consciences into balance with our thanks giving, we tend to feel depressed, guilty, for having been the one who found the dollar on the sidewalk! I wonder if the Pilgrims didn't feel the same way?

We're so philosophically and religiously oriented to giving, rather than to taking, that we scarcely know what to do with unearned, unmerited blessings. One thing we shouldn't do is depreciate them. One thing we can do is take them, marvel at them, wonder how best to use them. For the found dollar, too, represents the sweat of someone's brow and calls for thoughtful stewardship. In a sense, it is even more sacred than the earned dollar. One doesn't blow it on a chocolate sundae just because it's unmerited.

What do you do with a sunset? Take it, and be grateful that God built beauty into his world! What do you do with blossoms on your neighbor's tree? Enjoy their fragrance, which neither fences can shut in nor ownership dilute. We don't have to own something to enjoy it. We just have to inhale, look, hear, touch, appreciate, cherish. There will always be more that other people will own than I own, things that other countries than mine possess. Why not be thankful for what they've got, as well as for what I've got?

WE'VE limited our thanks giving to what we have, what we own, what we have fenced in. Why? There's so much more outside any fence than there is inside. The grace of receiving starts with the whole wide universe. It starts simply with looking up and exulting that it is all there and that we are all here to see it and say it!

Receiving is not easy because we are proud. Most of us want to pay back any and all favors received. We try, awkwardly, to do that even with compliments "paid" us. (We're not willing to so much as say "given" us.) Perhaps some of what we receive we can indeed pay back later, or to someone else. Much, though, we shall never be able to pay back. It is, for example, a futile gesture to argue with God over who shall pick up the check. And we do argue in all sorts of ways. "What can I do for you, God, now that you have done this for me?" we ask, to cover our embarrassment. The answer is nothing, absolutely nothing. Even our lives would be so little. Or we go off promising, "I'll do something for you sometime, God, really I will." But really, we won't. Really, we can't. And no use feeling guilty about it. All we can do is receive. All we can do is let our appreciation flow through us, out of us, to others. All we can do is be aware, and let our awareness sensitize and transform our relations with the other passengers on planet earth.

THE reception accorded a gift enlarges the gift and makes it holy, or diminishes and demeans it. Perhaps the reason that so much giving is so perfunctory is that so much getting is so perfunctory. It is possible so to receive a gift that it becomes priceless. "And it was so little," the one who gave it thinks to himself. On the other hand, who has not felt hurt, crushed even, when his gift has been downgraded or refused? It was the manner of receiving, in both cases, that made the difference.

Talk about techniques, if that were what one was hunting! The gracious receiver unwittingly makes the giver feel that his gift is too small, the ungracious receiver that his gift is too large.

But more than what "works" on the giver, what happens to the receiver is important. How great is our self-imposed penalty for being so self-sufficient that we cannot happily accept! "I will not come to dinner, because I cannot invite you to dinner." "I will not accept, because I cannot give." Giving—and receiving—must be more than tit-for-tat. "To whom do we owe dinner invitations?" a wife may ask, as if one were sitting down to write checks at the end of the month.

And no doubt there are dinner invitations in that category. And certainly the habitual sponger can create a certain amount of disenchantment. But graciousness does not keep a scorecard. And if it does, not only is giving not what is being done, but receiving is not what is being done, either.

We simply can't justify all the good things that come to us. We can't pay for them all, or perhaps even for most of them. We can only receive, growing smaller or larger by the way we do it. And when we worry about somebody's getting "something for nothing," let him who has never himself got something for nothing be the one to throw the first stone.

Faith As More Than a Delaying Action

WHY IS IT that conservative Christians seem to reach most of the same social conclusions and destinations as everyone else, only about twenty years later? It looks as if a sizable contingent thinks the Kingdom is licked and is merely trying to hang in as long as possible. For such, rearguard defense is the equivalent of stunning victory. In the evangelical lexicon, last one in is a good egg.

There are indeed some things that Christians do not or should not choose to do. But when we abstain while the parade goes by, only to fall in at the end, I don't see that life-or-death principles are involved. Tardiness and invisibility are not necessarily cardinal Christian virtues.

One of the reasons for Johnnies-come-lately to the outer world is a hangup on separateness. If you can stick to Rook while all about are playing bridge, you get a gold star. Or at least you did when and where I went to college. A rearguard action is still being waged on that one, I rather think, but as far as I know, attendance at motion pictures is no longer cause for instant academic excommunication. What happened was that "Hollywood" so infiltrated the living rooms of the elect that everyone became hard put to it to explain the difference between the little screen and the big screen. It boiled down, they decided, to the individual's concept of personal Christian stewardship, which is where it should have been all along. Even bowling became legitimate. (Maybe part of the trouble was that they used to call them "alleys.")

When I was a boy, I was not permitted to catch ball on Sunday afternoons. Inside the house, I could do almost anything that did not make noise. I no longer feel the sharp sense of guilt nurtured then, and have even been known to weed the grass on Sunday afternoon (quiet), though my conscience would still balk at letting me shingle the roof (noisy). But having waged those and other rear-guard actions so long in company with a host of Christians, readjusting my rationale as I went ("Is it work or is it play?" "Is it free or do I have to buy a ticket?") and discovering that it didn't seem to have much to do with the coming of the Kingdom one way or the other, I have begun to wonder what is the virtue of being last? Is the task of the Christian simply one of benign footdragging? How many cultural patterns, habits and outright prejudices are we defending in the name of God, when God may not be that much interested, or is not, at least, by the testimony of our belated actions, as interested as he once was?

We like to use the expression "cutting edge" to describe where the action is and where we should be, and I am rather sure the cutting edge is not on the hindside. The excitement of spiritual commitment, it seems to me, is not in being last where everyone else has been, but in being first where no one else has ventured.

If firstness and lastness applied only to the standard once-evangelical sins, maybe they wouldn't matter too much. But when they apply to the involvement that can—and will, with or without us—make this a more just world, I do not think it is the better part of Christian valor to be last over the fence. The delaying-action psychology of faith in some areas has made us timid and protective in all areas. Faith was meant to make us bold and free—not simply doggedly hanging on but confidently radiating hope.

40

You Just Can't Get There from Here
(But You Can Get Somewhere from Here!)

A LOST motorist stops by a lone house and asks directions. The householder, after several attempts, gives up. "You just can't get there from here," he decides. We chuckle, thinking that anybody can get to anyplace from anywhere. In a car, maybe yes. In a life, maybe no. Part of the problem with a life is that we become different people as we go, more often than not changing intentions and destinations. Another thing is that we can't go down to the auto club and get a map for a lifetime or even for a year's worth of living.

Any time is a good time for us, young or old, to ask, "Where do I want to go? What do I want to become? What do I hope to do with my life, or what is left of it? For even though age has a way of narrowing options, most of us have more than we realize. But being President is not necessarily one of them.

Many of our ambitions are so grandiose that we're just not going to get there, let's face it. We're not going to get global peace or eliminate poverty or exterminate greed next week. Man, you just can't get there from here, and it doesn't seem to me heretical or fainthearted to say so.

In fact, there are some goals that I am not sure you can reach at all by trying to reach them. This has been part of our religious and social delusion. Some of the most significant goals are by-products that we achieve almost incidentally. Too often we have neglected doing what we could do where we were for trying to do what we couldn't where we weren't. Not that every need is close to home, but it is easy to become so ritualized about an errand of mercy that one rides roughshod over people on the way to it. If an ambulance kills someone as it proceeds to an accident, it seems to me we're not really coming out ahead.

But most of us are immobilized by immensity, by the sheer bafflement of getting to where we want to go, even if we are sure of where that is, which is not usually the case. The secret is that you *can* go somewhere. One thing leads

41

to another in all sorts of unexpected, unmapped and unmappable ways. I have the feeling that God never gives out all the directions at once.

I graduated from high school during the Depression. College was not even a possibility at that time. I needed a job because my father was out of work. Jobs were scarce. I went to see a family friend who was an executive in a big company. There was nothing available, but because I had a home print shop and was interested in printing, he sent me to the letter shop that did their work. They had nothing but sent me to their typographer. They had nothing and that Friday I went home discouraged. Over the weekend I received a special delivery letter from the typographer. "Go to the Ruud Water Heater Company," said Edwin H. Stuart (I shall never forget him). "I think they have a job for you." And I got the job—not because I tried to get it or even knew it was there, but because one thing led to another.

You can get *somewhere*, even from here, any here. And who knows but God, it could become all that you ever hoped for, and more!

If I Should Wake Before I Die

WHEN I WAS A CHILD I thought as a child, I prayed as a child. Though there have been numerous revisions of childhood's classic "Now I lay me down to sleep," I prayed it nightly in the version which used the line: "If I should die before I wake, I pray the Lord my soul to take."

Only now does it occur to me with how much more alacrity we pray at sundown than at sunup, from childhood on. It is almost as if we assume we can get through the day without outside assistance, but need help getting through the night. Man's primitive terror of darkness and isolation rustles and creeps in that nursery petition. Who knows what lifetime fears have been nourished by its nightly bedside use, to be buried, eventually, deep in the subconscious?

And yet, I think, the greater psychological and spiritual damage was more subtle. The mistake—which was one of emphasis—has continued to dominate the way we think about life and faith. It is that the thing in the childish prayer that seemed important, the thing with clout, as we would say now, was dying, not waking. It was dying that put the fear of God into us, not waking. Waking, we assumed, was the normal procedure, and dying was the out-of-the-ordinary event that would interrupt it. So we took waking for granted and dying not for granted. We still do.

Haven't we sort of turned around the probabilities? It is a lot more certain that we shall surely die than that we shall fully live. What a change in outlook there would be if we believed that waking required more attention than dying. For it is clear that most of us have never wakened, really wakened, to the shining wonder of life, to our unexplored and mostly untapped personal potential, to the full freedom of faith, to the zest of here and now. Some of us never shall, and what a waste of God's creation it will be to die without ever coming close to becoming the man or woman one could be. There are so many in peace and war who never have the chance or the choice. So many of us who do have, act as if waking is just something one does if nothing else happens in the meantime.

How long has it been since you were really excited about *being here*? I must admit that I'm not one of those early-bouncing types who springs out of bed at the first click of the alarm clock radio. I like to get gradually accustomed to being awake, even to setting the clock a quarter of an hour early and then savoring those fifteen snug, smug minutes before I roll out. But the day is where work and opportunity lie for most of us. It is the day which the Lord has made—and after the first half hour I do my best to rejoice and be glad in it.

But so much of the time I feel as if I am running on

fewer cylinders than there must be in there somewhere. What, I sometimes wonder, would happen, *could* happen, if I were ever really, totally, utterly, fully, awake? What would happen if I were wholly committed to life, alert, sensitive, excited? This I do know—it would be the most revolutionary thing that ever happened to me or that could ever happen to anyone.

At this point, I am supposed to say modestly, "Well, it *has* happened to me," and then tell you how it can happen to you. But all I can suggest is that we both pray the terribly grown-up prayer, the one in which all our longing and imprisonedness reach to the Liberator who is within and beyond and around us and who beckons us on, "If I should wake before I die!" It is surely a prayer to be reckoned with.

Bump

IT WAS one of the traditional, yellow highway warning signs. It said, "Bump." Sure enough, a hundred or so feet later, there was a bump, but we were prepared and were not caught by surprise when we drove over it. We wouldn't have been surprised anyway, for we traveled that road frequently and the sign and bump had been there for at least three years. Instead of eliminating the bump, the highway repair people had put up the sign. And the sign, which one would suppose to be a temporary warning until the need for the sign could be eliminated, had become a permanent installation. Somebody had accepted the bump as a normal condition and decided that if travelers were put on notice, all responsibility was fulfilled.

It's bad enough when this happens to highways, but it's worse when the technique is used to cover the unrepaired, unregenerated places in our lives. All we have to do, we seem to suppose, is to warn people about our less commendable traits, and from there on it's up to them. "I have a short temper," we say. "You have to remember that I fly off the handle." Or, "I have trouble getting along with people." Or whatever. Having put up the "bump" sign, we feel no responsibility for the bump itself and no compulsion to do anything about it. It's as if admitting to a shortcoming—better yet, publicly confessing it—is an acceptable or even desirable alternative to getting rid of it. "Bump," we announce humbly, then almost proudly leave the bump where it is.

I suppose that part of this grows out of the new emphasis upon honesty and openness in human relations. We try to level with each other. We're told we must accept people for what they are, not for what they can be or what we think they should be. If we are supposed to do that for other people, the argument tends to go, why shouldn't they do it for us? One reason is that morally and ethically we need to be harder on ourselves than we are on others—perhaps one of the most distinguishable marks of the Christian. (The reverse, which is to be seen more often, is certainly not a supremely Christian trait!) The Prodigal's father can accept in his son what he cannot easily accept in himself. "Knowing thyself" for what unfortunately you have been is one thing, but for what with resignation you expect to be is something else. A "bump" sign is really no shining indication of honesty, but a declaration that this particular shortcoming is now a closed subject. "That's the way I am," we say, as if saying it covers a multitude of sins when it doesn't cover at all but reveals. Revealing is an excellent starting place, but a poor finishing place. There are no traits, no qualities of temperament, no habits, no moods that are off-limits to the gospel. And none of them is redeemed simply by the admission that it is there.

A "bump" sign, if it is to be used at all, should indicate that something better is on the way. It is an announcement of improvement and not a substitute for it.

"Well, you know me," we apoligize to God and to God's children. He or one of them might well respond, "Yes, I sure do know you. So what now?"

How Will I Do As a Cold Christian?

WILL WE love God in January as we did in July? How will we react when our faith comes home to roost? We've been saying all these prodigal years, "A man's life does not consist in the abundance of his possessions." Now the abundance that made it a believable statement seems suddenly to have disappeared. Will there be mutiny off the bounty? Did we, do we, really believe what we were saying? Or will it become obvious that we were putting more trust in things than in God, who placed the oil deposits where he wanted them?

There's nothing that reveals men's souls like the law of supply and demand. We are experienced at being Christians out of our surplus. Can we be Christians out of our deficit? It is one thing to praise God in a room that is heated in winter and air-conditioned in summer. How will we do when the reverse is true? Suppose gasoline is rationed and the week's allotment ridiculously small—what will we embarrassingly discover about our personal priorities?

Oddly, our government did little to prepare us for lean years. And I am beginning to wonder how well the church prepared us. There, too, we have been conditioned to be consumers, users-up, rather than conservators. We didn't replant as we went.

There is certainly no virtue in hardship, pursued in and for itself, for that way lies as much shallowness as can be found behind insulations of luxury. Hair shirts, whatever they were, once were thought to be good for the soul because they were grievous to the body. Even physical and mental flagellation has been practiced for its supposed spiritual benefit by those who believe they had no right to feel comfortable when there was so much of evil and hurt in the world. I can see how under certain conditions there can be cause-to-effect relationships, even misguided ones. But I am not convinced there are valid effect-to-cause relationships. That is, by putting on a hair shirt, I don't think I work backward into penitence or remorsefulness or whatever was supposed to come first. By dancing in the aisles, I don't think I can counterclockwise produce the spiritual elation that, at least for some people—King David, for one—manifested itself in dancing before the Lord.

There is a point here somewhere which is illuminated by the story of an order of nuns founded on a strict vow of poverty. Purchased as part of their identifying garb were shoes that were the least expensive to be found. As years passed, these cheap shoes no longer could be had. In order to duplicate them, they had to be made by hand at a very high price. Habits, at least of that kind, have been discarded for the most part, but the counterproductive habit of trying to work ourselves into something in reverse is one we haven't kicked.

So it seems to me that becoming better people by the simple technique of living with thermostat down or gasoline tank low doesn't have anything much to recommend it. But neither is it the end of the world. It was Paul who told the Philippians: "I have learned, in whatsoever state I am, therewith to be content." Or, as the New English Bible sharpens it: "I have learned to find resources in myself whatever my circumstances." Either way, perhaps the key word is "learned," and even Paul had to do that. If we now put our minds and our faith to it, perhaps we can, too.

See That Parking Lot?
It's Where I Went to Church

I DON'T MEAN IT WAS a drive-in church, one of those places where worshipers are sealed in steel cocoons and where "Honk, If You Love Jesus" might well be a liturgical response. But then one can be cocooned in his own preoccupations and priorities in a church pew, too. Either way nowadays, it is possible to come as you are and leave as you were.

No, mine was a dress-up, walk-in, sit-down church where you could lean over to whisper good-morning to someone you knew and loved and who, simply by being there, helped to make it church for you. On the front wall was a marble plaque memorializing an early pastor and paraphrasing a verse from chapter 12 of Daniel that, Sunday after Sunday, burned itself into my boyhood: "They that turn many to righteousness shall shine as the stars for ever and ever."

But now the church is gone—torn down to make way for what they call progress, in this case a parking lot. I think the plan is eventually to extend a wing of an adjoining hospital onto the space, and that will be better than a parking lot and perhaps than a church that had outlived its address. I have often wondered where the marble plaque went to, but with the church gone, I guess the words couldn't burn their way into today's adolescent dreams, anyway. There was an immense prism'd chandelier in the center of the high church ceiling, magnet for the eyes of generations of babies lying on their backs on cushioned pews below. I suppose it didn't look like much when they got it down; it probably ended in a junkyard.

I am not that old, but already so much of my life has been torn down, and so much of American life, and while we are richer for some of it, I think we are poorer for much of it. Vast chunks of Pittsburgh itself, where the church was located, have been demolished, to be rebuilt in glass, concrete and aluminum. Some said that tearing it down was the best thing that ever happened to Pittsburgh. When I go back to visit, the city looks new and shiny. But the landmarks are gone. These days, it is easy to get lost.

The office building in Philadelphia where I spent seven years of my editorial life was a hole in the ground the last time I went by. When I go into New York City, which is not very often, I check to see if the old Christian Herald building is still there on 39th Street. I find assurance in the fact that it is, though it is occupied now by strangers.

Change is a part of the human condition. But I must confess that when I visit Jerusalem and see houses built into and along and inside the ancient city wall, and know that these houses have sheltered people for hundreds of years, they give me a sense of firm foundation that our disposable houses do not give. Perhaps those who live in the ancient rooms would prefer more than I that they be modernized, and that may be the problem. Who wants to live in a landmark? Landmarks seem to be valued mostly by people who prefer to live and work and worship somewhere else. The old church was torn down because, literally, it could not be "kept up." Those who had the meaningful memories left, taking their memories with them.

Could this be what is happening to America? Too many wanting the landmarks saved but making no contribution by a meaningful presence to the saving?

It Doesn't Say,
Ye Are the Sugar of the Earth

THERE IS a time for salt and a time for sugar. Sugar is not a salt substitute, nor vice versa. I learned that dramatically one morning when I was having breakfast at the counter in our kitchen. My wife keeps a green glass covered dish filled with salt on the countertop, for easy access in cooking. The sugar, also on the counter, is in a blue plastic covered dish. That morning when I was having coffee, I absentmindedly uncovered the wrong dish and put two teaspoonfuls of salt into the coffee, along with a generous portion of milk. My general position on coffee is that one should have a little coffee in his sugar and milk. Taking a hefty sip, I knew instantly that something was terribly wrong. The salt concentration approximated that of the Dead Sea! What I needed in my coffee was sugar, not salt. Grain for grain, pound for pound, we use a great deal more sugar in life than salt. Dentists and medical doctors keep reminding us that it is easy to use too much sugar. As a chocolaholic myself, I know how it is. Many a time I have groped my feverish way to a Hershey bar, to drown my sorrow in a gulp of chocolate and almonds.

But let's think about sugar as a component of the Christian life. How important is it, and have we gone overboard or underboard in the sweetness-and-light department of faith? I have the feeling that some of us most of the time and most of us some of the time act as if Christians were intended to be the sugar of the earth. What the Bible says is salt, not sugar, and the two are not interchangeable, as I discovered with my coffee and as we sooner or later discover in our religious lives. Most of the time, we may be trying to substitute sugar for salt. We have forgotten that what makes sugar interesting is contrast. Anyone who has eaten a meal in Pennsylvania Dutch country knows about sweet and sour. The one heightens the other. A meal in which everything is sweet—say, pancakes and syrup— leaves you satiated and sticky. There is a time to have— and to be—a sour pickle, though only for balance and contrast. The problem is that sour pickle types tend to be sour pickles all the time, and sweet types tend to be sickeningly sweet. I used to hear the country proverb, "You can catch more flies with honey than with vinegar," which is true, if flies are what you want. What isn't pointed out is that it could as well be stated, "You can *kill* more flies with honey. . . ."

Now, it may be that there are spiritually diabetic Christians who are so addicted to non-stop smiling and beaming countenance and smother love that their friendly neighborhood theologian should put them on a sugar-free diet for a while. (Substitutes aren't the answer, either, for when people talk about a "saccharine" personality it sounds worse than if they had said "sugary.") For the rest of us, sugar in moderation is not only a good thing but a part of the well-rounded Christian personality. There are so many bitter experiences in life that can be sweetened, for self and for others, by the right word or concern at the

50

right time. There are occasions when "I love you" is exactly the right thing to say.

But we don't have to smile constantly, world without end, not even if we are gospel singers. There is a time to weep as well as to laugh. Sweetness is no substitute for saltness. But sugar is nice to have so many times, even if not all the time, to provide added enjoyment along the way.

II. Looking Around

Listening — the Other Half of Communicating

THE BIG WORD these days is communication. "We must communicate!" we are told on every hand. We hear about the "breakdown of communication" in families, in marriages, between generations, in government, and the implication is that if and when this happens, you have virtually had it. But in all these worried exhortations, communicating is almost always assumed to be talking, making noises—if only grunts from in front of a television set. When that is all that communication is understood to be, no wonder it breaks down. For this doesn't take into account the other half of communicating, which is listening, receiving, hearing grunts and all. Listening is actually the more important side of communicating, as any happily married wife who has the ability to hear more than her husband is saying will testify.

You can go out and take a course in public speaking, and it's a good thing to know how to do. But who is teaching a course in public listening—or private listening, for that matter? And yet, effective listening may accomplish more than effective speaking.

Some years ago when I was in India, the telephone rang in my room at New Delhi's Ashoka Hotel, and the voice said, "This is Prakash Jain to see you." Thus began one of my own more dramatic adventures in listening.

A few weeks before in New York I had received a letter from this gentleman, who wanted to write an article for *Christian Herald*. He was by religion a Hindu, by profession a journalist who had studied in the United States for the three years just prior. I wrote back and told him it happened that I would be in his city in three weeks, and perhaps he could come to the hotel to see me. We were then publishing a series of articles about nonmainstream American sects under the general heading, "Toward Understanding," and contemplated widening the series to include other world faiths. Our theory was that the writer best qualified to explain a faith would be one who was a follower of it.

There in my hotel room we talked for more than an hour. Mostly, he talked, responding to my questions. "How do Hindus justify having several gods?" I asked. He replied, "How do Christians justify it? We have three aspects of one god—god the creator, god the sustainer, god the destroyer. You have God and Satan and Jesus and the Holy Spirit, and then some of you have, in addition, Mary and all kinds of saints. For you, God and the devil are competing deities. For us, their qualities are part of our one god." He said a good deal more than that, but this was the gist of it.

Then I got around to the favorite tourist topic—sacred cows. "How come?" I wanted to know. To him, it was perfectly logical. "We believe that all of life is sacred, but obviously, you have to eat something. So we chose one animal to symbolize all animals. We chose the cow because it is the animal whose milk provides food, that works with us in the fields, that is closest to us." I wasn't ready yet to feel wholly tolerant toward the lumbering beasts wandering around town at will, but I could see the point.

JUST before my visitor left the hotel room, he said something that I found terribly poignant. This man who had lived and studied in the United States, who knew us and our ideas so much better than we knew him and his, made the traditional Hindu "praying hands" good-bye gesture, and said, "You are the first American who ever listened to me."

I was telling that story to someone later on, and the person asked, "Did he listen while *you* witnessed to him?" I believe I did "witness" that day—by hearing him out. For one thing, I witnessed to the fact that I respected him and his effort to understand the universe, and that I valued him as a person and fellow human being. There may well be a time to talk, but just because time is limited—or perhaps especially when time is limited—talk is not necessarily the way to communicate. And what, anyway, is the Christian trying to communicate? Is it not, "God values you"? If I had not cared enough to listen to what mattered most to him, why should he have thought the God I believe in would care, either?

There may be a place for cold-turkey testimony, but it seems to me that it puts quite a burden on the Holy Spirit and very little on one's own holy spirit of compassion, concern, caring. If you want to communicate, care. Caring *is* communication, with or without words.

I remember the story told by Evangelist Fernando Vangioni of South America at the 1966 Berlin Congress on Evangelism. He had held a meeting in New York City at a Spanish church and a number of men and women responded to the invitation. As is the routine at such meetings, these "inquirers" were then shunted to a back room for "instruction." A young woman in the group demurred, perhaps feeling trapped by the technique. "You can't do anything for me," she said. "I'm no good. I don't want to hear any more preaching."

"Let me just pray for you," said the evangelist. "Then you may go, if you wish." She couldn't very well refuse him that, and so he prayed. So moved was he for this disillusioned young woman that his voice broke and tears ran down his face. "I've prayed," he said presently, wiping his eyes with some embarrassment. "You may go."

She looked at him strangely. "I will stay. You have wept for me; now you may talk to me."

So many people don't adequately care, even some of us who are going through the motions, saying what we think we are expected under the circumstances to say, lovelessly dispensing the appropriate clichés. And we think we are thereby communicating the gospel of the caring Christ!

It is a phenomenon of our age that it is possible to make a very good living at listening for pay. There is, of course, more to it than that, but what a psychiatrist does in large part is listen. That's the time-consuming part of his job. That is what many of his patients need most—simply someone to listen, someone who will not try to have the last word or go into shock over what is said, or preach, or moralize. For so many Christians who do condescend to listen do it merely as preparation for pouncing.

Paul didn't say it in I Corinthians 13, but he might well have said it: "Love doesn't insist upon having the last word."

SOME people who listen—including, I fear, some Christians—get their kicks that way. "Now tell me all about it!" they urge, reveling in every juicy tidbit. The good listener doesn't drool. He—or she—listens not for what he will hear but for whom he will hear. Perhaps there are so many professional listeners because there are so few qualified amateur ones.

Listening will not solve everything. After months during which American youth complained because nobody in government would listen to them (some officials made a public point of not listening), somebody in Washington discovered that, after all, listening didn't cost anything and you could often disarm dissent by listening and then go on and do as you pleased. That kind of listening will not get one very far for very long. Listening is a commitment

58

to personhood. It is not to be entered into lightly or unadvisedly. It may shatter your preconceptions, leave you vulnerable. But in a very real sense, for Christians, vulnerability is the name of the game. We have made faith into a mighty fortress, a shield and defender, when compassion, caringness, listening, require a venturing out of security, a lowering of shields, a laying down of swords and spears while someone's wounds are being bound up. Just as love makes a man or woman most vulnerable to hurt, so does respect for life. But where, in the long run, does security lie? Are we secure when we are imprisoned by our fears inside the walls?

Communication has two sides, telling and hearing. We've assumed that our only mission was telling. Part of our mission—and perhaps it is the larger, more influential, even more Christian part—is listening.

Why Stop If No One's Coming?

ONE of the big things wrong with this country is that our reflexes are gone. Our good reflexes, that is. Our moral reflexes. Our reflexes of selflessness, compassion, general decency. Except for a few holdouts, most of the Watergate participants regret now what they did then and wish they hadn't done it. If Chappaquiddick were to be rerun, does anyone suppose it would happen in the same way, or at all? What separates the men from the boys is not coming to the right decision in leisurely retrospect but coming to the right decision at the split second a decision is demanded. The events which most dramatically reveal the souls of men and of nations are those which do not allow time for the weighing of pros and cons, which cannot wait until the votes are in or the dust settles. I believe that more is wrought by reflex, for good or ill, than this world dreams of.

The engraving process is a laborious and often frustrating one, whether it's churchgoing, the private disciplines of faith, the cultivation of the good, the true, the just. At some unexpectedly crucial moment of our lives, all that we will have going for us will be what we have already built into the circuit. It will make the decision for us, carrying us into right or wrong, courage or escape, greatness or oblivion, and all we will be able to do then is stand and watch.

How Goes It?

WHEN SHIPOWNERS were making their last great bid to hold onto transatlantic passenger traffic, the Cunard Line used the advertising slogan, "Getting there is half the fun!" And it was. Maybe even three-quarters. Shipboard travel, unlike no-nonsense jet transportation, was not just a way to get to your vacation—it was part of your vacation, and a large part.

When it comes to religious and moral destinations, we haven't paid as much attention to the niceties of travel as we should have paid. We haven't generally considered the getting there to be any fun at all, or even a factor to be taken into account. It was the other-worldly result that counted. How you achieved the result was a part of this world's doings, where very down-to-earth rules applied.

In our family, when our children were small, we made a photo Christmas card each year with the youngsters in a Christmasy pose of family togetherness and joy. I am now chagrined to admit that taking those pictures was accomplished only with great emotional bloodshed. One or more of the children quickly tired during the long session; I, the photographer, would become irritated; four happy smiles would be momentarily and unanimously assumed

In so many areas of our public and private lives, because we have so few securely built-in certainties, we have lost the saving power of spontaneity. Before we do anything, we have to figure out whether, this time around, we want to do it, or how it's going to look, and by then it's too late. There are some decisions we should never have to make more than once.

Which brings us to stopping at stop signs. Drives there a man or woman with soul so ordered who has never barreled up to a stop sign when nothing was coming and wondered what was the point of stopping? The point was and is that stopping at a stop sign is a better habit to get into than not stopping at a stop sign. The point is that at some intersection there *will* be something coming, and that if you wait until then to get the habit, you may not have the time or the mental alertness to hit the brake.

My own reflexes have been seriously wanting at times, but more than once they have saved me while driving and maybe a couple of other times, too. You know how it goes. A child or perhaps a squirrel or cat or chipmunk darts across the road in front of you, and your foot, as if it has a mind of its own, leaps to the brake pedal before your mind can say "squirrel!" Your reflexes take over the driving so instantaneously that you are almost a bystander.

On the moral roads we all travel, it seems to me we're coasting through more and more of the stop signs when no one is coming. Reflexes grow dull against the fateful moment when they will need to be sharp. A confrontation comes suddenly, and you can't react fast enough, automatically enough, to cope with it. We have said "No one's coming" for so long that when someone does come, when a life-changing moral issue erupts, when reputation or survival or character is on the line, there's no resource ready to take over. We are most revealed in our reactions to crises we cannot predict.

Reflexes in the making so often seem wearisome, and unnecessary. The routines that engrave micro-miniature circuits by the millions in our brain, don't just happen.

61

only after much snarling by me. Everyone was immensely glad when the picture-taking event was finished for another year. Producing that scene of peace and goodwill was anything but peaceful and generated about as much goodwill as a dogfight. What I remember now when I see those angelic pictures is the excessive spiritual cost of getting them.

There was a classic statement made during the Vietnam war by a U.S. military man who observed quite seriously that it was necessary to destroy certain villages in order to save them—an attitude more lethal but no more stupid in principle than I was exhibiting at Christmas, or than so many desensitized Christians are displaying in their almost ferocious pursuit of righteousness. The cause of the trouble is that we are result-oriented, and by result we mean successful result, and by successful we mean what appears at the moment to be desirable. We measure an evangelistic campaign by the number of countable converts, not by the faithfulness with which the gospel was preached or whether it was indeed the gospel that was preached. We get to the point where we think the measurable result is all that counts and that the way in which the result is achieved is so unimportant in comparison that anything goes. The financial problems of many overextended religious entrepreneurs have occurred because goals somehow became more important than means. History is littered with the bones of men and women and children who to someone with power seemed less important than the grand objective. We are still reaping the bitter harvests.

Surely in our pursuit of faith we cannot be faithless. Surely in our pursuit of honesty we cannot be dishonest. Surely in our pursuit of righteousness, we cannot be unrighteous. Being on our way home is no justification for tramping through a flowerbed.

For the Christian, getting there should be not only a substantial part of the "fun" but is assuredly a substantial part of the responsibility. The question is not just, "Where are you going?" but "How are you going?" The way we are able to answer the second question may have a great deal to do with the way we are able to answer the first.

The Sin of Committing Discouragement

"WHERE SELDOM is heard a discouraging word," we once sang happily in four-part harmony, home on the range or in the small town or city suburb or urban high rise, as we glowed with all that is spacious and brotherly and best about America. These days, it seems to me we're hearing discouraging words more often than not, and speaking them, too. I don't think we realize how serious it is to diminish someone's courage, which is what discourage-ment means. I don't think we realize the awesome importance of the Christian's intended role as encourager, giver of courage, and the frequency of our actual role as discourager, corroder of courage. For courage or discourage is not something one usually gets or loses in solitude, but in company with or because of others.

In Acts 28:15 there is an interesting statement about courage. As Paul was on his way to his trial in Rome, something happened that made him feel better. "When the brethren heard of us, they came to meet us as far as Appii forum and the three taverns; whom when Paul saw, he thanked God, and took courage." Contrast that with what happened when the Children of Israel were on their way to the Promised Land (Deuteronomy 1:28): "Whither shall we go up? our brethren have discouraged our heart saying, The people is greater and taller than we; the cities are great and walled up to heaven; and moreover we have seen the sons of the Anakims there."

Discouraging anyone is not only petty thievery of the spirit; it is a spiritual felony. It robs a man of power to endure. Who steals my courage takes my very life. The

63

man or woman who is discouraged is put down, bled of strength, immobilized. It is the privileged duty of the Christian, of all people, to give strength, not to sap it; to give heart, not to dishearten. How incredibly accusatory to have to say, "Our brethren have discouraged our heart." How incredibly sad ever to be one of the brethren of whom it could be said. Discouragement kills the spirit which makes survival possible. For example, parents who downgrade their children are pulling from under them the very rug on which they must learn to stand if ever they are to stand tall.

"Whistling in the dark" has been casually dismissed as an exercise in futility. But what's wrong with whistling in the dark? It sure beats whimpering in the dark! When I was a boy, a friend of mine lived down the road, around the bend. I spent many evenings at his house, for he had an electric train set long before I did and he also had lots of postage stamps to trade. It doesn't seem far now when I go back for a visit, that distance between our two houses, but it seemed forever then, especially when I walked home after dark. To the right of the bend was a wood—dark, unfriendly, mysterious and brooding at night. I walked fast, my ears so sensitized by fear that I could hear mosquitos turning over in bed. Heart thumping, I prayed my way home. And I always made it!

These are times for praying, for whistling and for laughing—gifts of faith. These are not times for cringing, for doomsaying, for longfacedness—by-products of unbelief.

Whatever I can do to build up another person rather than to tear him down, whatever I can do to strengthen another's spirit rather than to weaken it, whatever I can do to make a man feel bigger than he is rather than to make him feel smaller than he is—these are among my most important tasks, and yours, for such a time as this.

Faith tells us to take heart! And to give it.

Peace Has to Have People in It

AT CHRISTMAS, more than at any other time of the year, we talk of peace. Hopefully, glibly, we talk of peace. Christmas has peace built into its bones. The sentiment of the first Christmas greeting—"and on earth peace, good will toward men"—has become a part of the Christian heritage and, for most of us, of the American tradition.

And yet, year after year—certainly this year—to speak of peace as if we had it, or indeed ever seriously expected to have it, is our principal annual orgy in innocence, perhaps hypocrisy, possibly blasphemy.

Why is this? Is Christmas decreed to be only a wistful reaching that reminds us of how far from God we really are? Is it a sentimental addiction for which we need a sort of Christmas Anonymous to keep us in the real world? Do we have to devise a theology that spiritualizes peace, makes it compatible with unpeace?

Or is there more here than meets the eye, something we are missing? For a starter, it seems to me that one reason our Christmas peacemaking has a fantasyland quality about it is that we simply are unwilling to accept the fact that peace must have people in it. Without people, we may have something—solitude, perhaps, or majestic splendor or the forest primeval—but we can hardly call it peace.

If it seems incredible to you that we could be leaving people out of peace, ask yourself, as I have been asking myself, what you think of when you think of peace. Close your eyes and think peace. What do you come up with? As far as I'm concerned, the pictures that come to my mind are ones that are remarkably untouched by human intrusion:

• A stand of snow-clad firs rising silent and aloof above virginal drifts unmarked by footprints (or snowmobile tracks).

• A mountain lake whose still waters mirror surrounding peaks with such clarity that were a photograph taken, you would scarcely know which was object and which was image.

• A sunset or sunrise casting highlights and shadows over the immensity of the Grand Canyon.

• A beach tideswept of sand castles and all other evidence of human habitation.

These are the pictures—every one of them uncontaminated by people—that say, "Peace!" to most of us. That's the kind of peace we celebrate on so many of our Christmas cards and in so many of our religious concepts. We achieve peace simply by taking out the people. Then there are no problems, only beautiful landscapes and seascapes and escapes. And to us, that says, "Peace!"

But isn't taking people out of peace a Christmas cop-out? Or a Christian cop-out, for that matter? How did we ever suppose that peace without people in the picture could be anything but phony? Now, I like lakes and mountains and spectacular scenery as much as the next person, perhaps more. I find something immensely healing in a panorama of rolling hills and natural magnitude—when I am in the picture, when I am there, when I am the intruder, the invader, the despoiler if only by footprint and breath and dislodged pebble. I confess that I would be turned off if a mob of people were there milling around me, horning in on "my" view. And yet they would be people with the same fears and hopes and rights as mine. Our Christmasy view of "Peace," then, always has us in the picture, but not other people. We are the beholders, and to behold, we must be there, if not in the picture, then taking the picture.

"Ye shall be as gods," a man and woman were told long before anybody heard of a little town of Bethlehem, and we have been trying to collect on that campaign promise ever since. We take godlike views of so much of life, assuming stances and vantage points for ourselves that we are not willing to grant to others, regarding ourselves always as the lookers, never the looked-at.

We do it at Christmas, too. We wrap a shattered world in solemn stillness. We pretend that sleep is deep and dreamless for everybody. Like a housekeeper cramming everything into drawers and cupboards when unexpected company rings the bell, our kind of Christmas sweeps everybody out of sight and therefore out of trouble. Christmas is our unique depopulation bomb.

And that isn't how it was at all.

Christmas, which is to say Incarnation, was God's way of saying, "Where people are, that's where I live. When you want me, knock at the door behind which you hear the sounds of sorrow or the silence of loneliness. Where there is despair, look for me there. Find a brother and there you will find me."

Christmas didn't take people out of things. Christmas said that people are what it's all about. Is it any wonder, then, that we have not done a very good job with peace, when we try to take people out of it? When we try to cover with a snow job the season most dedicated to people?

Suppose we visualized people when we talked of peace. All kinds of people, including those elbowing us for breathing space on the street and in the world. There's a good place to practice peace, and Christmas is the ideal time to start.

Another place where peace would be better than what we have now is on the highways, where we so readily revert to jungle cunning and savagery. For most Americans, a workable peace will have to have not only people but automobiles in it.

Peace will come, if it comes, not only bumper to bumper but father to daughter or son, husband to wife, child to parent. Close-to-home peace is sometimes the most elusive peace of all. It will not come without respect for personhood. One of the tragedies of our time is that when we subconsciously dream up an idyllic Christmas peace, those who are biologically closest to us may not be in the picture at all.

Peace on the street, in the community, in the city—how

do we achieve that? How do we ever get to the point where we feel as secure, as wind-free, in the peopled places of life as we do in the unpeopled ones? Maybe it's just that we have never tried to make a Christmas card out of a slum. We've moved Christmas off somewhere else. If we moved it back, who knows what might happen?

"Behold, I bring you good tidings of great joy which shall be to all *people*."

To Eulogizers of Unleaking Pipes

"WHY DON'T YOU TELL US what is right about things, instead of what is wrong with things?" So ask aggrieved Americans, aggrieved church members, aggrieved any-bodies. And there is a real danger in becoming an expert in the care and feeding of gloom. The person who habitually points out the dark lining in every silver cloud can take the joy out of anything and everything.

What makes me think about prophetic criticism is a conversation I had with Dr. Ernest T. Campbell, then preaching minister of The Riverside Church in New York. Someone had put the "Why don't you—?" question to him. His concern as a minister, he replied, had to be with the one brick askew rather than with the ninety-nine bricks perfectly aligned. Which is a scriptural position. Jesus pointed out that it is the sick, not the well, who need the physician, and that the caring shepherd leaves the secure flock while he looks for the one sheep that is lost.

It's also a pragmatic position. When a water pipe in our house springs a leak, I do not customarily say to my wife, "Say, have you noticed those thirty-seven pipes that are not leaking? They are really doing a great job, aren't they?" No, I do not say that. I yell, "Quick, a bucket—and what's the telephone number of the plumber?"

When an alarm is telephoned to fire headquarters, the operator does not chide the caller, "What are you so excited about? We have 11,731 houses in this town that are not burning." Nor does the caller preface his cry for help with a genial statement about how nice the town is, how filled with pleasant homes, clean industries and good schools, and how, though he hates to trouble anyone, the house next door is on fire and something should be done about it. Not at all. Almost incoherent with anxiety he shouts, "Help! The house is on fire!" At the moment, this is all that matters. The tranquility of the 11,731 is simply not germane at that point.

One compelling fact of life is that it takes very little to wipe out a lot of tranquility. To sit up at night with a wet basement can dim, surprisingly fast, twenty years of peace and quiet. Perhaps that is not logical, and certainly it isn't in the long run, but that's the way life operates in the short run. Another problem is that leaks and fires and political ineptness and social unawareness cannot be neatly contained. They not only do damage beyond themselves if neglected, but they indicate inner rot.

The pipe, for example. When one goes, it's a good sign that others may soon be going, too. The leaking pipe is a tip-off to the general health of the other pipes, however placid they appear to be on the outside. The fire may well be a clue to some precaution that needs to be taken to prevent other fires. The failure of a church or denomination or community or family or nation to be sensitive to even one need, one hurt, one tragedy, says something about its state of health.

Alarms are practically always for a minority plight, be it fire, leak or injustice. No amount of justice can remove the need to be concerned about one injustice. Until that one fire is out, that one leak fixed, there is no time for a eulogy of houses not burning, pipes not leaking, people not hurting.

Of *course*, there is a great deal that is right about America, right about the church, right about our institutions, our traditions. But when something is wrong, that's what needs action. One leaking pipe is one too many.

Doesn't Anybody Live Here Anymore?

WALK DOWN any street and you get the feeling that the people you see are just passing by. Their interests—and ours—seem to be somewhere else. Once we were a nation of builders. We have become a nation of users. These days, nobody seems to own America. Not so long ago, everybody did. We are throw-away people living in throw-away buildings on throw-away streets in throw-away towns. Chewing gum wrappers are the least of our litter!

Maybe that's why some American cities are among the dirtiest in the world. Maybe that's why buses and subway cars of New York and Philadelphia (to name two cities), not to mention walls of schools and public buildings, are marred by scrawls of many colors and off-colors. For those disposed to leave their mark, the spray can has been the greatest technological breakthrough since the invention of lipstick. "Let us spray" has become the compulsive call to worship of the great god Graffito.

Most of the fuzzy spray inscriptions, in New York at least, include names of individuals—pathetic pleas for immortality. It's as if someone were shouting, "Hey, somebody, anybody, this is my name! I'm here! I'm alive! I'm me!" The advantage of the bus or subway car over the stationary wall is, of course, the incomparably wider circulation.

Because we are spiritually and sociologically rootless, we are no longer content, departing, to leave behind us footprints in the sands of time, to be swept clean by the next tide. Today's transient in heart would rather leave footprints in somebody's freshly laid concrete.

Every village and hamlet suffers and inflicts its own defacements. Broken windows. Overturned gravestones. By the side of the road, garbage by day and the sightless eyes of discarded beer cans by night. Huddled masses of billboards, each yearning to shout free, turning breathtaking scenery into obscenery. The problem is that ecology and esthetics on the one side and economics on the other have in our system acquired an entwined relationship. The dilemma inherent in the American way of life is that we must eat our cake in order to have it.

Pride of ownership would help. It has become almost embarrassing to sing or listen to the song, "This Is *My* Country," but it is, and it had better be, and when any of us loses the words, we all lose. But there are two kinds of ownership—the sharing kind and the possessive kind. We have been historically programmed for the latter. We have forgotten how to enjoy what we do not possess. We have tried to make a buck at the expense of someone else instead of at the gain of someone else. Enduring prosperity must come out of the overflow, not out of the undertow. It comes by serving others, not by serving self. It is a happy side effect of caring.

We might as well face the fact that we and our children are going to be around for a while. Believing "This Is My Country," and making it possible for all Americans to believe, we could make the best of it. The very best.

It Will Be a Great World
If They Ever Get It Finished

EVERYWHERE I GO, things seem to be pretty well torn up. We appear to be living in an excavation. The voices of the air hammer and riveting gun are heard in the land. Detour signs disrupt our comfortably learned habits. Regiments of monstrous machines gouge green hills, laying bare the bones and tendons of rock, all to speed the going. Disembodied overpasses cure in the sun; waiting for unrolling interstate highways to catch up.

Large sections of inner cities, devastated at first by neglect and then by intention, are being rebuilt. Every major airport seems to be having, and giving, growing pains.

Where is the college which does not have at least one new building in progress, the surrounding campus in dusty disarray? Every town has at least several substantial street repair jobs going on at any given time. In Manhattan, the power and light company apologizes for its burrowings in busy avenues with the cliché, "Dig we must for a greater New York." In Kaohsiung, Taiwan, my taxi edged through a construction zone and encountered at the far side a placard in English, "End of crash area. Resume speed."

Not only are places and things torn up. So are ideas, even those we encounter in church. Some traditions that once were important no longer seem to be of the same importance. Other beliefs that once we had little occasion to think about now claim a great deal of our attention. Most of us are uneasy, unsettled, mixed up, confused, though we try not to be any of these. Where are the landmarks?

Maybe it's just that we are facing up—perhaps for the first time—to what are the doctrines on which we would be willing to stake our lives. Whatever we have said we believed, the times are revealing our priorities with ruthless clarity. When the chips are down, our instincts for self-survival embarrass and dismay even ourselves. It may be that we have too long looked upon faith as a way to keep the chips from ever getting down.

Well, anyway, we console ourselves, someday we will get back to normal. It will be a great city, a great highway system, a great world, a great liturgy, a great church, if they ever get it finished. But will it? Unfinished-ness is, I suspect, the normal human condition. When you and I finally settle down, it will be six feet down.

Living a life is something like reading a book. There are, I suppose, people who read simply to find how the story turns out. But most of us read, at least in substantial part, for the joy of the reading. Proof of that is the fact that the more absorbing the book, the sorrier we are to come to the end, even if everybody does live happily ever after. It's not so much how the story turns out that provides the zest and excitement, as it is the story itself. If the reader lives only for the ending, he's not getting as much as he should be getting out of the reading. A book, a life, is for savoring as you go, word by word. "I have come," said Jesus, "that men may have life, and may have it in all its fullness."

Maybe it *will* be a great world if they ever get it finished, though I don't think I'll be here then. But maybe I can help to build it while I am here. Building is more fun than complaining, any day.

Where Do We Go from <u>There?</u>

IT HAS OCCURRED TO ME how seldom we think of there, any there—which is to say any long-range goal. We are most of the time concerned about here, any and every here—which is to say any short-range goal. Of course, we walk one step at a time and the next step is the only one over which we have immediate control. But next steps relate to where we hope to get to sooner or later, and where we plan to get to determines or should determine next steps.

All that seems very elementary. It is only when we put it into practice that it becomes complicated. For the fact is that although we are taking steps that may lead us where we want to go right now, they are not necessarily taking us in the direction we hope eventually to go. I have the feeling that many of our problems would be solved if, instead of asking, "Where do we go from here?" we asked, for a change, "Where do we go from there?" Where do we go from wherever it is that the decision we are making at this moment will take us, and can we even get to where we really want to go from there?

A number of the problems of our country could be better handled, it seems to me, if we wondered a little more about there and a little less about here. For example, whatever else Watergate and the tape transcripts and the whole mess revealed, it certainly revealed an inordinate preoccupation with the immediate. The most shocking thing about the tapes was not the expletives that were deleted, but the future that was deleted. Apparently nobody thought to ask, "Where do we go from there?" Where could we have gone from there?

Desperation always turns to the immediate. If you're hanging on the edge of a cliff, you understandably clutch any available handhold. To turn it around, obsession with the immediate is the measure of desperation. The man or woman with no saving long view, with no time or inclination to ponder steps after steps, is desperate beyond words or thoughts.

Losing sight of the future is responsible for so many of the mistakes we all make. It is when we begin to think that the present is all there is that we lose hope and with it judgment. When the waves are so high that all we can see are waves, it is easy to think that waves are all there are. In a crisis, only a long-range view or a clear memory of one can sustain us.

Every time I travel by plane, the ground, buildings, vehicles and people 30,000 and more feet below look unimportantly Lilliputian. It is knowing that I have to return to earth and be again one of those Lilliputians that keeps my delusion of grandeur and my sense of disproportion short-lived. The President—any President—will someday not be President but will have to come down to earth. Where does he go from there? The person who is insulated by power or wealth from the grim realities of life will one day find the insulation wearing thin. Where does he go from there? A hasty marriage or a sudden divorce is one way to go from here, but where do the parties go from there? A solution may seem ideal at this moment, but what are the implications, the expectations, the fallout? Where is my solution taking me and do I really want to go there?

I don't know about you, but I'm going to try to remember to test my reactions by posing the question to myself:

"Where do I go from there?" For *there* is going to be a lot bigger than *here*.

What Kind of Faith Will the Traffic Bear?

THOUGH THERE MAY BE small areas of our lives which seem detached from what is going on around us, there are surprisingly few events and emotions which are totally personal and private. What happens to us affects others, and what happens to them affects us. Yet so often we assume there's just God and I, and that he can deliver the blessings I seek—security, peace of mind, contentment, fulfillment, prosperity—without any of this spilling over onto some undeserving neighbor.

This franchise approach to faith looks for God to keep the faithful one fail-safe as part of the contract and expects God to prepare a table before him in the wilderness in the presence of his enemies, a Psalm come to life. There are indeed magnificent and largely untapped resources of inner-stability available to the faithful in the midst of instability. But if you're looking for literal tables of bounty to which you may have access while your enemies do not, it's easy to figure out what produced the enemies in the first place.

The prayer we most often and most unthinkingly pray, begins, "Our Father." Thus you cannot get beyond the first word of a prayer without finding a brother and taking him with you the rest of the way. To come to God at all, we would seem to have to admit that we do not have exclusive claim upon him. Have we considered, I wonder, that prayer may not after all be a form of preferential cloud-seeding, and that, seeded or unseeded, the rain falls upon just and unjust? Then what's the advantage to the just? Perhaps the advantage is not in the blessing but in the ability to recognize the implications of the blessing. Putting all of life together and finding that it spells God may be the discovery through which confident living lies.

If ever I need additional evidence about the rightful scope of personal petition, I get it every time I drive a freeway, thruway or turnpike during rush hour. To pray upon setting out, "Lord, protect me and mine," doesn't really constitute adequate coverage. In order to protect me and mine, the Lord must also protect them and theirs. Let an accident or even a flat tire block one lane, and instantaneously a throbbing traffic jam begins to build. As cars screech to a halt, the line between motionlessness and motion flows backward from the blockade. The effect is soon felt miles distant.

Sometimes I have had the heady experience of driving in the opposite direction, seeing such a jam developing and watching motorists heading toward the tie-up with unwitting abandon. Meanwhile, ahead in my lane, the same kind of immobilization may be reaching out to wipe the contented smirk off my face.

All of which indicates that the only prayer that makes sense on a busy highway is a prayer for all who travel, myself included but hardly more than incidentally included. For if someone—friend, enemy, known, unknown, rich, poor, little, big, black, white—beside or before me has trouble, I too am going to have trouble.

Maybe it wasn't such a big problem on an oxcart road in an oxcart world. But when great concentrations of humanity are rushing here and there at high speeds inches apart, then I am at the mercy of your judgments and you are at the mercy of mine. We had better pray for each other.

Interrupt Me!

THERE ARE orderly ways of doing things. Schedules, timetables, deadlines are for most of us a necessary part of life. The person who flits haphazardly from one unfinished task to another is disorganized. Past a certain point of disorganization comes an inability to perform. Trying to cope with fourteen different demands clamoring for attention at one time can throw the whole motor system into neutral and we call that a nervous breakdown or a mental crackup. "Don't interrupt me!" has become an important defense mechanism so automatic that in an effort to preserve our sanity we are in danger of missing much of the excitement and fulfillment of life.

For the way it works is that the most significant experiences generally come as interruptions. The orderly procedure is suddenly shattered. We had the day mapped out, and something unanticipated occurs, changing the schedule and often our life with it. One secret of buoyant and effectual living is staying limber enough to accommodate the unexpected.

Jesus knew how to do this. When children intruded upon his presence, the disciples, self-appointed protectors of the person and majesty of the Master, were immediately uptight. There wasn't time in their schedule for anything but the serious business of taking Christ to the nation. "Scoot!" they said, not necessarily because they didn't like children but because they didn't like interruptions. Whereupon Jesus said, I think in an easygoing drawl, "Suffer the little children to come unto me, for—" and turned the interruption into not only one of the most memorable sermons of his ministry but into a happy benediction without which his church would today be poorer.

Can you think of anything good that ever happened to you of a size big enough to remember that was *not* an interruption? Have you ever wondered what other things tried to happen for you and to you that you wouldn't let happen because you didn't want your routine disturbed?

We say, "Don't interrupt!" in so many different ways. Perhaps it's a child trying to get a word in edgewise when we adults are having what we like to call a serious conversation, and we think it's more important to teach the lesson of noninterruption to the child than the lesson of awareness to ourselves. It is so terribly easy to put out the light in a child's eyes, and it is a light you—and he—cannot turn on at will. Perhaps our teen-agers do not talk to us because we made them wait too long.

Need does not keep a schedule. Though a riot or a revolution may offend our sense of orderliness, there it is, either to transform or be transformed. Telling a hurting human being to come back when you have time, is to insure that when you get around to saying, "All right, my good man, what can I do for you?" he will not be there. He will be out making it on his own, in all the disillusioned, desperate ways that people make it.

How many of the miracles of Jesus were scheduled in prime time? I can't think of one that wasn't the result of an interruption. It turned out to be a miracle because he stopped, turned aside, listened, paused, felt, wept. What miracles might have happened and didn't happen because you and I were too tidily self-centered to do any of these?

David and Bathsheba and the American Dream

IT'S REALLY TOO BAD that the X-rated details of the story of David and Bathsheba so captivate our attention that we miss the PG and even G implications. That is to say, we've been so absorbed in the way it explicitly describes somebody else's sin that we have missed the way it implicitly describes our own. There are several reasons for this, no doubt, but among them are two that I find especially intriguing. The first is that the story makes us virtuous voyeurs, seeing what we normally are not expected to see and seeing under the best of auspices. The second I suspect has something to do with the name of the lady involved. If the story had been about David and Hoglah, say, it wouldn't have had quite the same zing. To put the record straight, the "Bath" part of Bathsheba means nothing more than "daughter of." Sorry about that. The "sheba" part means "much value." So that Bathsheba—like most daughters now but not all daughters then, when sons were more welcome—was the pride and joy of her parents and they memorialized their happiness in the name they gave her.

I do not need to refresh your recollection. David not only had sinned, but had committed murder in an attempt at a kingly coverup. So we come to the prophet Nathan and our place in the story. Read for yourself the early part of chapter 12 in 2 Samuel. Here Nathan accuses David. He does it not by speaking directly and immediately about the sins of adultery and murder, but about the sin of supposing one occupies a privileged status that people less valued by God are obliged to support.

As Nathan spins his allegory, he uses two characters, one rich and one poor. The rich man has almost everything. The poor man has only one lamb. When the rich man wants to throw a party, instead of reducing his own substantial lamb inventory, he takes the poor man's lamb, kills, cooks and serves it. David, not recognizing himself as the villain, is righteously outraged. What he won't do to the heartless rich man when he is caught! After letting David fume for a moment, Nathan says quietly, "Thou art the man." David, caught in his own decent indignation, is shocked and repentant. "My God, have mercy upon me!" (Psalm 51) might well have been his next words.

Though adultery and murder may not be sins of which we are guilty, we are not off Nathan's hook. When we begin to think that we are special people who don't have to live by the same rules or even in the same world that other people do; or that we are a nation that has a God-ordained right to global resources that other nations do not have by the same divine right; or that it's perfectly reasonable for all of us or some of us to have as much food as we wish while others do not have as much as they need; or that because we are Christians and/or Americans the world owes us a living—that ever-present, ever-shattering accusation, "Thou art the man! Thou art the nation!" brings us back to reality.

The sin that is at the root of many others is the sin of arrogance, of literally taking for granted, of assuming that I am entitled to God's top-heavy blessings simply because I am I.

David repented of his sin. I am not sure that we are yet even aware of ours.

The Loneliest Question: Is Anybody There?

MY younger son is an amateur radio operator—a radio "ham," as they are called. He has talked to amateurs as far away as Asia and Africa and as close as the next street. A parent can't be exposed to this sort of thing for very long without picking up some of the vocabulary and general excitement.

For example, finding somebody to talk to. If you've made arrangements with someone to listen, that's a "schedule." If you don't have a schedule, what you do is start sending the letters CQ, followed by your call letters, which in this case are WB2ZCH. You keep on sending CQ, CQ, and your call letters. Then you listen. If anyone has heard who wants to reply, the signal comes back, WB2ZCH, and the acknowledging station's call letters. Thus, contact is established, and a conversation begun (they call it rag chewing) that may last a half hour or more. (It takes an especially long time to say anything in code!) But often the CQ call is in vain. Nobody is listening. Or there is too much interference. Or the hearer is hunting bigger or more distant game. Or nobody wants to bother. The sender of the CQ never really knows who might be hearing him. All he can go by is the response that he gets. One of the great joys of amateur radio is hearing somebody reply, "You're coming through 5-9-9," which, being translated, means, 'I'm getting the message and it's loud, clear and readable."

How the letters CQ came to be used for this purpose, I do not know. Judging from some other radio amateur code abbreviations, I wouldn't be surprised if once upon a time it had something to do with "Seek you." Anyway, that is basically what it means. Is anybody there? Will somebody let me know I am not alone? I am seeking you.

How many CQ's, I wonder, are being sent out every day—and I'm not talking now about amateur radio, but about our amateur living—that are never answered? How many unscheduled cries of loneliness are being transmitted in one kind of code or another, and nobody is responding?

How little, sometimes, our craving for human response requires. Two cars approach each other in the darkness. One driver dims his lights and the other responds in kind; there has been a momentary acknowledgment of each other's needs, of mutual dependence. You are asked for a quarter by a man on the street, and you give it with a slight pressure of hand upon outstretched hand—a momentary admission of human worth and that the two of you are somehow bound together in this thing called life. The pressure in the hand warms both of you; money alone may be the cheapest, easiest gift of all.

There are so many people in this world who simply want their existence acknowledged. "See me! Hear me!" they are pleading in all sorts of ways. Sometimes theirs is the loneliness of a crowded street, or of a church or of a family. But we are not tuned in, or we're not good enough at whatever the code happens to be, or we're wrapped up in our own problems, and we never get the message.

We can't help *everybody*. But wishing we could is what makes it possible for us to help *somebody*. One of the most terrible of tragedies, I think, is to be a Christian and never hear a lonely cry.

A Pharisee's Thanksgiving Prayer

IT TOOK me some time to figure out the real difference between those two men who went up into the temple to pray. One, you will recall, was a Pharisee, the other a publican. A Pharisee was a professional good guy. A publican was a bad guy; he collected taxes for a cut of the take, an arrangement that tends to produce instant corruption. Watch carefully as Jesus switches the labels.

The characters come onstage. The action begins. The Pharisee finds a well-lighted place and prays thus with himself: "God, I thank thee that I am not as other men are, extortioners, unjust, adulterers, or even as this publican. I fast twice in the week, I give tithes of all that I possess." He is singing all the stanzas of "How Great I Art."

Then the spotlight shifts to the publican, standing off in a dark corner. The publican does not lift up so much as his eyes unto heaven, but smites upon his breast, saying, "God, be merciful to me a sinner."

The surprise comes when Jesus points out that we should take our cues not from the Pharisee but from the publican. The traditional roles are suddenly reversed. Why? What did the Pharisee do that was wrong? What did the publican do that was right?

Was the Pharisee's fatal error that he had prayed "with himself"? Some versions indicate that what is meant is that he, to pray, stood off by himself, which pretty much shoots that one down. Anyway, those who pray with or to themselves aren't likely to know that this is what they are doing. They may, in fact, be the most fervent, passionate, articulate pray-ers of all. Well, then, if it wasn't that, was it his self-centeredness? Would his prayer have been more acceptable if he had majored in how great God was, instead of how great he was? There could certainly be something in that, but not because God has to be buttered up. The notion that God waits until he hears the right passwords before he picks up the hot line at the Throne of Grace creates his ego in the image of ours. I am not so sure that it matters all that much to God who gets the credit. He knows the facts, in any case, and I cannot believe he is interested in twisting our arm until we cry "Father!" But our self-centeredness can indeed make a shattering difference in us and to us. When we get to the point of assuming that we deserve our blessings, we're goners.

And so the moral is, of course, that anyone who exalts himself shall be abased through his own blinding euphoria, and that he who humbles himself shall be exalted through his sensitive awareness. The question is how does one humble oneself at a table heaped with turkey, cranberry sauce, pumpkin pie, the works? What kind of prayer does one pray at a table like that? Too often it is some variation of "We thank thee that we have merited these blessings and we beseech thee that we may continue to deserve same."

The point we tend to miss is the importance of recognizing kinship. The Pharisee was glorying in his unlikeness. The publican was admitting to his likeness. Thanksgiving is not the time to deny kinship with the human condition. It is the time, perhaps more than any other, to ponder it. We dare not pray the prayer of the separatist, "I thank thee that I am not as others are, hungry, homeless, without hope, illiterate, wretched." How, in God's name, can a Christian face bounty in a world where it is so unevenly distributed, without praying the prayer that makes him vulnerable, "Lord, be merciful to me a sinner"?

Prophecy and Christian Conscience

ONE of the first criteria by which some Christians seem to measure a war is whether it relates to the fulfilling of biblical prophecy. Some parts of the world, even for those who make a religious hobby of prophecy, appear to be somewhat out of the prophetic mainstream and provide material for only oblique inferences, usually drawn from the godlessness of whatever side we oppose. A conflict in the Middle East, on the other hand, causes an immediate outbreak of exposition, explanation and justification by those who claim to be prophetically knowledgeable.

I think there are two things wrong with this kind of prophetic preoccupation. First, it presumes that it is possible to fit current events with precision into the prophetic picture, or vice versa. Massive superstructures of speculation have been built upon some very slim scriptural foundations, and one gets the feeling that events, even of the most tragic sort, which seem to confirm a particular theory, are cheerfully greeted by that theory's proponents. This brings us to the second thing wrong: To accept the premise that an event fits a prophetic projection tends to remove it from any scrutiny of the everyday moralities of the event. The perfect license for nonchalant acceptance is to convince yourself that God is calling the shots. Put yourself on God's side, prophetically speaking, and then you do not have to make any judgments on your own or even show any compassion for or understanding of the participants. This state of mind dictates that whatever contributes to the "fulfilling" of prophecy is right and just and whatever obstructs it is wrong and unjust. In my estimation, such an attitude, far from being proudly and confidently Christian, is ignominiously sub-Christian.

Each time there is an outbreak of hostilities between Israel and her Arab neighbors, there is a rash of Bible-quoting and misquoting. Some prophecy pushers evidence almost sadistic satisfaction that "the end time" is near or at least nearer, and that the Battle of Armageddon is shaping up nicely. If that's the way it has to be, their philosophy goes, there's no point in trying to bring peace, not to mention justice—or even to explore what constitutes justice—for to do so would be to tamper with the divine will.

Armageddon, or whatever passes for it, must not come aided and abetted by me. The Christian is not in the Armageddon business. For him, hope springs eternal. When his obsession becomes the destruction of all the

84

supposed ungodly, he is a sulking Jonah not only out of touch with those whose deliverance is his mission, but with God. Sometimes I can't help wondering why the prophetic bad guys at any given time seem to coincide so neatly with our own self-interest. Antichrist always belongs to some other race or political party or nation than our own. I have not heard of a fair-haired, blue-eyed antichrist, though I could be wrong on that, for the list of nominations down the years has been long.

How does the Bible stand on prophecy without conscience? "It must needs be that offences come, but woe to that man by whom the offence cometh." In that kind of probability there is no protection for accomplices or even bystanders.

Perhaps in the Middle East, as elsewhere, we could get a just and compassionate and therefore Christian perspective, prophecy or no, if our first question was not "Who is right" but "What is right?"

Take the Worry Out of Being Close

WHY must we be wary of each other? Why are we so afraid to reveal ourselves? For one thing, the more people there are in a given space, the more the need for psychic or emotional or even physical privacy. Everyone has to have a place, visible or invisible, into which he can withdraw at times. Everyone needs doors that can be shut and sometimes bolted, even against those closest to us.

But we Christians have overdone it. So many of us are going through life in a holy haze, seeing nothing, hearing nothing, feeling nothing. Even the good that we would do we prefer to accomplish by remote control—by prayer, if possible. We don't want to get personally involved—because we feel inadequate in the face of a particular need and assume there is someone more adequate who could do it better; because to be involved is to share whatever the hurt is; because to become involved is to be forced to accept another human being on equal terms. To avoid those risks, we stay at arm's length or town's length or world's length.

I am beginning to realize that there is really nothing much of value we can do at arm's length. We hear about how doctors, nurses, lawyers should be "professional," which is often translated to mean that they must not become emotionally related to the one being served, and that clergymen must act this way, too. And every clergyman has conducted funerals at which he would have wept had he not steeled himself. But have they and have all the rest of us steeled ourselves too much, become too emotionally rubber-gloved? Have we worried too much about being close?

In the biblical story of the healing of a man who had leprosy, the account says, "Jesus touched him." Perhaps Jesus could have healed the man without touching him. Or perhaps, just perhaps, the touch, at risk, was a necessary part of the healing process. How effective can be the ministry of anyone who is frightened or repelled or disgusted by the one to whom he proposes to minister? We've taken the touch out of truth.

At the Bowery Mission in New York City, one of the sights that never fails to stir me follows the altar call, to which ragged, unshaved, unwashed men often respond. As they kneel, the pastor kneels alongside and puts his arm across the shoulders of one man after another, by that one act acknowledging him as a brother. There *is* healing in a touch.

So much of the warmth is going out of the world and even out of our faith. To stop a blaze in a fireplace you separate the logs. To quench the production of energy in an atomic reactor, you pull out certain rods, separating the fissionable materials. Warmth requires closeness. When we walk a crowded street, we so often do not look into other eyes, lest some signal of recognition should flash back. We are desperately afraid, it often seems, that we may find a brother with some claim upon us.

What takes the worry out of being close? I suppose it is the quiet admission that I am no more God's child than others; that they have a passion to live, as have I; that they are on their way somewhere as I am; that they bleed as I bleed.

More of this world's hurts than we dream of could, I suspect, be healed by a touch. Perhaps by yours.

The Christian Celebrity System

EVERYBODY needs heroes and probably always will. Maybe my trouble is simply that I have never had any interest in asking a star—movie, sports or otherwise—for an autograph. Perhaps that is why the star system as it today relates to the Christian arena, also eludes and baffles me.

I respect talent, and I respect dedication. But I'm a little wary about exploiting either and especially about exploiting one against the other. A great singer who sings for God is not doing God any particular favor. Must we constantly reassure ourselves, by featuring big-name testimonies, that God is for real? We won't take it on the say-so of the garbage man, but let the word come from an astronaut, and wow! As things stand, the vocalist whose recording has sold a million copies makes a more promotable religion star than the quiet little lady in the church choir who may have lived much closer to the sharp edges of life's hurts and joys. He has a talent and she hasn't—but a talent for what?

And as things stand, the impact of one's witness seems to be in direct ratio to the vileness of one's pre-born-again adventures. By lapping it up we are almost demanding of the person who ever expects to amount to anything as a future Christian that he earn in early wild oats credentials that will later offer adequate contrast. The best trick of all is to use the pre-b.a. state as a time in which to accumulate mammon that may be enjoyed post-b.a. without let or hindrance—all that and heaven too! It was, however, a ploy that didn't work for the rich young ruler.

Most of us did not come into the Kingdom clothed in either wealth or glamor. Is that why we are awed by those who do? Speaking of worldliness, I think we Christians are never more dazzled by the bright lights than when we turn them on, or are turned on by them, in the sanctuary.

There were no celebrities when the faith began. A band of men had been challenged to be what they had never been, a challenge and a becoming that reached into every space and every moment of their lives. The disciples were, if anyone was, "stars." Yet this was never exploited by the disciples themselves or whatever passed for their public relations department. Except for a couple of lapses, they were glad enough to forget what and where they had been.

Suppose they had done it our way. Take Peter, the big fisherman, for example. After pondering how to make his reputation work for Christ, they might have put out a press release:

"This coming Pentecost, Peter will preach. Widely known as a former fisherman, his record catch—when the weight almost sank the boat—stands unbroken in the Northern Galilee Fishing Conference."

Or this, about one of the other disciples:

"Matthew, notorious tax collector who last year made a decision for Christ, tells how he formerly cheated for a living. Hear inside secrets that will enable you to save tax money."

I can't quite put my finger on it, but there is something that widely misses the mark when we make what was and is a dusty Galilean way of life into a television special. Maybe we should stop desperately hunting and using celebrities. I am not sure that Jesus seeks first the Big Man on Campus. Or what it proves when a Sunday-school teacher becomes Miss America.

The Other Side of Brotherhood

HAVE YOU EVER PONDERED how much of our involvement with other people, how many of our good works, how much of our religion, works out with ourselves having or trying to have the upper hand? However noble the original concept, our motivations can be easily captured by self-interest and self-gratification. Take, as an example, humility, which is supposed to be one of the less domineering virtues. Humility is sometimes practiced for pleasure and profit. Play it right and humility can get you farther, faster, than arrogance. But when it becomes calculated and self-serving, humility is one of the worst forms of arrogance. Righteousness, another excellent virtue, produces in its highly self-conscious form some of the most overbearing people on the planet. Hell hath no fury like that of a man who believes God told him something that God didn't tell anyone else.

Brotherhood is one of those great ideas which we have managed to subvert to personal advantage. The fact that we observe Brotherhood Month causes me to recall how savagely churches have fought over brotherhood, the dispute being whether all men are brothers, or whether only Christians are brothers. I suspect that some Christians have never mastered the second proposition because the first one was, for them, total heresy. I remember being disillusioned in boyhood when I heard one minister say of another from a different denomination, "He's no brother of mine!" He didn't believe in the brotherhood of brothers, let alone in the brotherhood of man.

Thinking back on that now, it seems to me that the trouble with that brother (if I may use the term), and the trouble with all of us to a greater or lesser extent, is that we regard brotherhood as a gift we have the option of bestowing upon some lucky recipient. What more beautiful way to bolster the ego than to say (most of the time silently), "Isn't it simply great of me, taking on this unfortunate character as a brother?"

Why is that our brothers, in the usual sense of brotherhood, so often come out looking like poor relations? "I get a little weary of well-doing, but, after all, he is my brother. When I give something to him, I can feel that I'm doing my teeth-gritting Christian duty." This could be called the "he's as good as I am" level of brotherhood.

Now, I have to admit that this motivation, however spiritually inadequate, has accomplished quite a lot. A contribution made out of a sense of obligation or even with a bit of arm twisting may indeed do some good, at least in the short run. But at this point in history we are coming to the end of a lot of short runs. One-sided brotherhood is no longer acceptable, not only for what it has done to the little brother but for what it has done to the big brother. Brotherhood is first of all a testimony to the fact that there is no big and no little. Brotherhood is not something to be conferred, but something to be accepted.

For it is not just that he is my brother. It is also that I am his brother. It is not just that I confer something upon him. It is that he also confers something upon me. As I assign him a relationship to me, I testify to my dignity and worth. As I relate myself to him, I testify to his dignity and worth.

That's the "we're in the same family" level of brotherhood. And I don't think we have reached it yet.

The Story of the Good Christian

IN THE STORY of the Good Samaritan, we identify with the Samaritan. Let's see how we would have written it—how, in fact, we are writing it. The two who pass by on the other side, doing nothing to help the traveler who was stripped and left half-dead, can be any two favorite villains. Our concern is with the hero—now, of course, a Christian—who drives by. That's us. Let's see how it might go.

Me (stopping car but staying inside): Wow, would you look at that? How did he get himself into that mess?

Holy Spirit: Obviously, he fell among thieves.

Me: Why didn't he look out for himself? Do I fall among thieves? No. Do people in my church fall among thieves? No. Anyway, I can't help everyone in the world who's in trouble.

Holy Spirit: He's not everyone. He's one man. And you're not everywhere. You're here.

Me: But I just happened to come along this road. What if I had taken some other road?

Holy Spirit: But you did come. And there he is.

Me (sighing and getting out of car): You down there! Can you talk? There's something I need to know—are you born again?

Man (weakly): I'm not sure about that. All I'm sure about is that I'm hurting.

Me (squatting down): I can see that your body is hurting. But the important thing is your soul. Have you given any thought to where you will spend eternity?

Man (more weakly): Right now, I'd like to get to a hospital.

Me: As a Christian, I ought really to be concerned especially with those of the household of faith. Only because of my better impulse will I take care of you.

Holy Spirit: Did you ever stop to think that maybe your better impulse *is* your Christianity?

Me: I'll help you into my car here. It's fairly new, so try not to get it all bloody. I guess you had better put on my coat. It will ruin the coat, but I'd look like some kind of nut, driving a naked man through town. Maybe you could scrunch down in the seat. (They drive toward hospital.) You're fortunate a Christian came along. You know that, don't you? Not everybody would have stopped.

Man: A couple of cars went by while I was lying there.

Me: Exactly what I mean. I guess you don't have any money on you. I mean, with no pockets, or anything.

Man: They took everything I had. I feel faint!

Me: Hey, man! Don't pass out on me! Wouldn't you know, he did. I didn't even get a chance to witness to him. Or to find out who's going to pay his hospital bill.

Holy Spirit: Doesn't the story say you pay the bill?

Me (sighing again): I work hard, am God-fearing and Bible-believing, and then something like this comes along! (Carries man into hospital.) No, nurse, I'm not next of kin. O.K., I'll sign for him. But there's nothing that says you have to give him a private room. Tell you what, I'll pay the cost for two days, and if he's not on his feet by then, he's on his own. I have to talk with the police, too? But I was just passing by—

Holy Spirit: That's the name of the game, isn't it—just passing by?

Praying When the Train Goes On

I THOUGHT of it one evening, as I was walking up the hill from the railroad station toward home. We live twenty-four miles north of New York, and for years I was one of some sixty thousand commuters who travel by train. Other hundreds of thousands travel by subway. All this may seem remote to someone living in a bright little town in Ohio within walking distance of work, but what I began to think about is as pertinent to where you live as to where I live.

You see, it was "my train" for those twenty-four miles. Then I got off at my station, and it was as if that train had never been. I forgot all about it, as I walked home. Some evenings I could hear its air horn signaling for a crossing up the line, but most of the time I was lost in other thoughts and heard nothing. Whether the train arrived at the next station was not my concern. I had made it home once more.

That one evening, how or why, I do not know, the thought hit me that other people, still on the train, were as anxious to get to their destinations as I to mine. We had made it this far, sweltering in summer, freezing in winter, and I would soon be home safe, but there was more beyond. Almost involuntarily, I breathed the prayer, "Grant them a safe journey the rest of their way."

For the train didn't exist just to serve me. There were others on it, and travelers who would board somewhere along the way and ride for a while. "My train" was as important to them as it was for a while to me. "Mine" became "theirs."

To ponder that I am not the center of some universe or other is a revealing thought. The journey does not end when I get off. Though my night comes on schedule, the day goes sweeping around the globe. Others are counting on it, even as I counted on it. I'm not sure that I ever before gave a thought to where a day goes from here. "How was your day?" my wife asks, and I never stopped to consider that it also belonged, and will belong, to others along its way.

There is something about time and space that is all of a piece. There is something awesome and divine about the trustworthiness, the dependableness, of natural law. To pray that "my train" may be early or late, fast or slow, to meet my personal convenience, is to ask everyone else along the line to fit into my schedule. Can we ever, in good faith, have the audacity to ask God to violate in our behalf immutable laws and functions of the universe, or expect him to take us seriously if we do ask?

A church does not exist just to serve me. It is not just "my" church. There are others who will wish to get on when I get off, some of them not yet even born. It was not just "my" college. Somebody made sure it was there when I wanted to climb aboard, and after four years when I left, the college was still going on, serving others. That college is worth a prayer and much more. It is not just my highway, my town, my street, my world.

Life is filled with things that are "there" when we need them. But the train, the plane, the system under which we live, the framework of society that supports us, came from somewhere and is going to somewhere. A man's journey is at best a small piece of the large journey that binds together all men everywhere.

Give a thought when the train goes on.

III. Looking Up

What's the Good Word?

THAT'S the jovial question that seldom gets an answer at all, and practically never an adequate one. In that respect, it is something like "How do you do?"—if we make a reply, we act as if the inquiry was "How do you don't?" for what comes out is a recital of ills and disappointments. We don't really have much to do with the good word, do we? We're much quicker on the draw with the bad word.

Why, I wonder, is it so painful to say something good about someone or some place or some experience? Why is it so automatically easier to say something bad? Is it because we think it shows more brains to see a flaw than not to see one? Or because people (ourselves included) wake up and listen to bad news, giving the news bearer a sense of power? Or because once you start in that direction, the worse the news, the better, in a can-you-bottom-this escalation?

Or perhaps we have been unthinkingly conditioned by what we thought was our religious faith but which was in fact our religious unfaith. We have a spiritual aptitude for taking great ideas and making them into little ones. We think that Christianity is most orthodox when it is a court for punishing offenders (generally with ourselves as prosecuting attorney), and somehow not as fully orthodox when it is a liberated life filled up and spilling over with joy. We think we are being defenders of the faith when many times we are only being pessimists. We forget that the Christian, by his very nature, just has to be an eternal optimist. And that his is not a do-nothing optimism but an optimism that motivates and inspires action—even when the action may seem too little and too soon.

I don't know about you, but I grow a little weary with overuse of such expressions as "last days," "end time," "end of the world." Faith is not preoccupied with ends but with beginnings, not with lasts but with firsts. The Christian optimist believes this is God's world and that betting his life on God is nothing to be afraid of. He is sure that God will have the last word, and that it will be a loving word because it will be God's. Believing, he can get on with the job. *That's* the good word!

Pessimism about the future makes us bitter and small in the present. We've corrupted even our good words, words like "honest," "frank." When you hear someone begin a comment by saying, "Now, to be perfectly honest . . ." you can be sure he's up to no good. Someone is about to be put down and sliced into little pieces. Why do we never preface with a preamble to honesty a recital of good qualities? I have yet to hear anyone say, "Now, to be perfectly honest, he's a great guy." But I have many times heard pious equivalents of, "To be perfectly honest, he's a scoundrel." Is honesty reserved for the worst? Is it not also for the best? Can we be frank only when we catalogue shortcomings? Can't we be frank with longcomings? We have embedded our judgmental pessimism into the very language! We have also embedded it into our very faith—and then have the presumption to call it faith!

So, what's the good word? The good word is that this is God's time and that you and I are privileged to be a part of it. To be perfectly honest, we not only should live with joy and magnanimity—we must!

Your Fingers Can't Do All the Walking

WITH APOLOGIES to the Yellow Pages, it ought to be said that the encouragement, "Let your fingers do the walking" does not necessarily apply to prayer and other aspects of the Christian faith. The assumption too often has been that all we had to do was clasp our hands and fingers in an approved Dürer-type prayer gesture, give God his instructions for the day, and he would take it from there. Prayer became the easy thing, even the lazy thing, to do, covering a multitude of sins of omission.

Before we go any further, humble and proper acknowledgment must be made of those saints of the Lord whose bodies are imprisoned by circumstance or physical disability but whose spirits wing free and whose prayers are a benediction to all of life. What an encouragement it is simply to be told by such a gentle soul, "I am praying for you." Some young people these days talk about vibrations, "vibes," good and bad. Certainly the vibrations from prayers of loving concern are worlds better than those from maledictions of suspicion, distrust, dislike and outright hatred.

But what we're thinking about just now is the pious use of prayer as an escape from involvement—as an escape from "walking." One of the great duets, soprano and alto, as I recall, that has stirred me as boy and man, comes from a passage from Isaiah set to music: "How beautiful upon the mountains are the feet of him that bringeth good tidings." At first I couldn't imagine that feet could be beautiful, nor could I see what mountains had to do with it. Then I realized it was the mountains, the personal effort, the mission at cost, that helped to make the feet beautiful. No fingers doing the walking there!

But prayer is not the only exercise in which our fingers can't do all the walking. We're adept at all forms of religious tokenism, at letting one labor-saving symbol or other do the walking. If we come up with a catchy line, we sit back feeling satisfied, as if we had done all there was to do, when we haven't really done anything at all. Take the motto, "In God We Trust." What a stupendous victory it was when we got that on dollar bills! Now we could let our currency do the preaching. Actually, when it comes to money—especially when it comes to money—more than a motto is required to make profession of trust in God credible.

In so many areas, in and out of church, we take refuge in ritualism, sacramentalism, worship itself, letting our tongues do the walking and our words, not our backs, do the burden-bearing.

It's interesting, isn't it, how many denominations were started because of disputes over the form or manner in which fingers should do the walking, and how few over the way in which feet should do the walking. Christians have quarreled bitterly over symbols in their desperate effort to escape the reality which the symbol symbolized. Instead of ministering as servants to the near and far needs of lonely, hurting people, it's more enchantingly "religious" to argue about theological presumptions that cannot be answered with finality anyway. The paradox is that it is when we are arguing, rather than when we are serving, that we think we are defending the faith. What we are in fact most often defending is some kind of actual or hoped-for preeminence.

When it comes to faith, it's more convincing to let your feet do the walking.

So What's Old?

THAT'S NOT the usual question. At least, until now it hasn't been. We've wanted, instead, to know what's new. If you think we have not had an obsession with newness, just read some of the package fronts as you wheel your way around the supermarket aisles. Product manufacturers work hard to get the word "new" on their labels. If it's old to start with, they throw in something so they can say, "New! Thermonuclear Power Added." Or they speckle it up so that you can see that it looks different, though what the speckles do is anybody's guess. People who study buyer motivation know that "new" is just about the most enticing word in the marketing vocabulary. As far as I can remember, I have never seen a package that brags about being "the same OLD" anything. In fact, did you ever think of how easy it is to put an exclamation point after "New!" but how you really have to force your hand to do it after "Old!"? But that may come too, the way the world is going.

For there are some things for and about which "new" is a totally meaningless word. When, for example, it comes to integrity in high office (or in low office, for that matter), we want the oldest brand we can get. We're not looking for someone who can invent a new improved formula of honesty—we've had some of those already—or a leader who has the cleverness to find loopholes that will let him legally do less than he knows he can honorably do. Aged-in-the-wood obstinate righteousness is old stuff, and some of it would look very good these days. The new improved concept of work, for another example, is downhill all the way—giving your muscle but never yourself. Ultimate payoffs always have to be in more than getting, because there will always be more that we don't have than that we do have.

Somehow, in life's lowest and highest moments we look for something old, not for something new. Every editor and pastor and greeting card designer thinks he must say something new and original at Christmas. But Christmas isn't new. It's old, and we might just as well admit it, for therein lies its joy and inspiration. Easter is another festival of the old—old thoughts, old encouragements, old hopes. How can one be sparklingly new about Easter, or why should one wish to be? In the deepest sadness of all, the death of a loved one, we search for the familiar, for the known, for the old. We are in the position of Peter, asking, "Lord, to whom shall we go? thou hast the words of eternal life."

Our obsession with newness was a part of our religio-patriotic prodigality kick. We no longer live in that kind of throwaway America. We're going to have to mend tears, sew on missing buttons, patch holes—in our faith and politics as well as in our shirts. Indeed, some of the young people are patching where there is not yet even a hole, and I was reading just last evening of how stores get higher prices for bleached, beat-up denims than for new ones. That way lies illusion too. I don't think we can have aging to order. You can't build antiques—you can only discover them. The sobering thought is that some of those old possessions we were so happy to unload as a generation's measure of progress—the round oak table and the rolltop desk—are now worth almost their weight in gold. Lots of old things and old ideas are.

Christ Is the Question

AT OUR HOUSE, we used to watch the television game show, "Jeopardy." Turning the tables, it supplied answers to which contestants then had to give the questions. Watching it made me think of the blithe statement we often hear, "Christ is the answer," and the rejoinder that evangelist Tom Skinner once made, "But what's the question?" That sounded like a flippant response until I began thinking about it. It didn't take much thinking to realize that if I don't have the right question, the answer, however impressive, will not make any sense.

Inventions, for example. There's nothing really new about nuclear energy. The makings have been around as long as the solar system. But the scientists who were on the scene in earlier times didn't recognize the answer when they saw it because they didn't have questions to go with the answer.

Going back further, take the wheel. It was an answer to a question about how to transport loads from here to there. Until there were loads to be transported, until man's mobility increased, there was no question. The "answer" was there all the time, waiting to be used. Inventions result from the right questions.

An answer is no answer at all until you and I have the question to go with it. That's why we respond to an idea, to a sermon, to a testimony, to a verse of Scripture, at one time not at all and at another time life-transformingly. We respond to the answer when we have the question to go with that answer. If we're lonely, then we begin asking questions about loneliness. If we're bereaved, then we wonder about separation from loved ones. If we sense that we're lost, we want to know how to find and be found. If life is falling in, we're ready for the answer on how to cope with life. Simply to say "Christ is the answer" is not especially grabbing unless and until I've got a question, and the questions come in many different ways and at different times and in different sizes.

But there is something more than that. If we don't need or think we don't need an answer at the moment, then maybe what we should be affirming is that Christ is the question.

How does a well-fed American Christian understand what it is never to have enough to eat? Christ is the question. We cannot be at peace with him and disregard world hunger. What about honesty in our business and personal dealings? Christ is the question. What about the motivations that cause us to spend our money for whatever we spend it on? Christ is the question. Our hearts are restless until they find rest in God because he never exempts us from the restlessness of questions and because Christ is the question.

It is not answers that drive us on, but questions. Answers allow us time to settle down, take it easy, assured that we have it all figured out. In questions, on the other hand, there is something of divine discontent, some heavenly uncertainty, something beyond, something undone, something insecure, some loose end. And there in our extremity, in our question, is Christ—not always as the answer or an answer, but as the Son of God, urging us to be what we have not been and more than we think we can be.

God Is Nicer Than I Am

"NICER" MAY NOT BE the best word for it. But I'm thinking of it in the sense that we say, "He's a *nice* person." And of course the word "person" opens up another whole box, because we aren't supposed to think of God in what they call anthropomorphic terms, which is to say, as a man. But even the Bible does that once in a while, and it is one of these whiles that reveals something not only about God but about ourselves. For, strangely, we are inclined to think that God is not as good, not as generous, not as thoughtful, not as caring, not as forgiving as we are. As so often happens, we have managed to turn completely upside down an impressive affirmation.

It is from the Sermon on the Mount. Jesus, comparing human fathers with God, observes that if a boy asks his father for bread, the father will not give him a stone. Or that if the son asks for a fish, he won't be given a serpent. Then follows this tremendous point: "If you, then, bad as you are, know how to give your children what is good for them, how much more will your heavenly Father. . . ."

How much more! What a comforting, heartening assurance. And yet by our actions and attitudes we so often make it read, "How much less." We seem to believe that God is capable of being much less loving with his children than we could ever imagine ourselves being with ours. How many broken men and women have groped their way through a shattering mistake or a tragic sorrow because they could not grasp that God was not only as loving or understanding as they were, but worlds more so.

A vindictive streak in the church is one of the major paradoxes of life. Because they assume God to be worse than they are, inquisitors of many eras and faiths have been less magnanimous than they had the capacity to be. What perversity in our natures, I wonder, so regularly encourages us to try to outdo God's sternness, but so seldom his love? Why is it that we justify our mercilessness in God's name, but our mercy in our own? ("I'm just an old softie," we apologize for our compassion.)

Was it an accident, do you suppose, that Jesus linked stone to bread, snake to fish? A stone resembles the flat round bread of the Middle East; a snake bears a certain resemblance to a fish. Was he saying that God has no cruel surprises up his sleeve, anymore than would any parent? That he is not capricious, is not a cosmic prankster, will never say, "Ha, fooled you that time"?

There is one thing more to ponder: that is the difficulty sometimes of recognizing a good gift when we get one. *How much more* God knows what is good and what isn't. "Good," from our point of view, usually means whatever is to our personal and immediate advantage. Even our limited kind of parenthood understands that. When a child asks for a loaf, he doesn't always get a loaf. Perhaps he gets part of a loaf. Perhaps he gets nothing. "It will spoil your supper," we sometimes say. Or if he asks for a loaf, he might instead get spinach. *How much more* wise than we are is God. What he gives will be good, as he in his eternal parenthood knows goodness to be, and as we on our microscopic platform in time and space can never fully comprehend.

How much more will God! We can rest on it to the very end. And then, too.

Worship As More Than Making God Feel Good

IN CHURCH, the question, "Why are we here?" is most likely to be asked when things are not going well. Perhaps attendance is falling off or receipts are shrinking or something else is happening to make the congregation introspective and self-conscious. For when there is zest, excitement, a sense of achievement, there is no need for asking, "Why are we here?" and no time for a church to sit around contemplating its nave.

When the question is sooner or later asked, the answer probably will have something to do with worship. "We are here in church to worship," is the answer we always seem to fall back upon when we can't think of anything else. "Worship" has become a sort of last-ditch reason for the existence of the church, especially in those bodies which have no strongly liturgical tradition. Worship, so the impression goes, is something you do in church when you run out of anything better to do.

This, it seems to me, comes from our distorted idea of what worship is, what it does, what it is for. The biggest distortion of all is that worship is something we do to make God feel good. The picture one gets is of God gratefully soaking up our praise and beaming approvingly. When, in this view, he does not receive the veneration and attention due him, he is out of sorts, at loose ends, and unfriendly to his creation.

This is a *Christian* concept? This adequately expresses the majesty, magnitude and glory *of God*? It strikes me, rather, as being a concept straight off Mount Olympus, with stained-glass windows added. Bending our effort to appeasing the wrath of an angry deity, to buying him off, to diverting his attention, to proving that we are not as bad as he thought, is nothing less than raw, primitive paganism.

"Look," this kind of pagan worship tries to say convincingly, "we like you, God. You're the greatest. Because we are saying so, God, we are the good guys. Those other people over there, those slobs who didn't even get up this morning and shave, who are not worshiping or even admitting that you exist, they are the bad guys, as you can plainly see."

Do you seriously suppose that the God of the universe, the God who holds the whole wide cosmos in his hands, the God who is the ground of our being, could possibly care? I mean, *you* wouldn't even care! The very thought of God keeping the books on who said or thought what about him, or keeping an attendance list on who is in his pew on Sunday morning (and, depending upon the church, Sunday night also), is demeaning to God. It contradicts the best we know about man, let alone about God.

Is this to say, then, that worship doesn't matter, one way or the other? That anything goes? That there are no rules for anything? Of course it is not to say any of these things. Worship matters a great deal. But it matters in a quite different, much more basic way.

If God is the same, yesterday, today, tomorrow, then he doesn't change. He doesn't blow hot or cold. He is not whimsical. If he doesn't change, who does? We do. We are the ones who change. Our worship doesn't do anything to God, but it does something to us. What it does is enable us to relate to forces that are there whether we relate to them or not, and by relating, to become more sensitive, more aware, more whole, more fully human.

God does not spend his time turning on and off faucets or pulling switches that enable the water of life or divine power to flow to where the water and light bills are paid up. He simply *is*. The water simply flows. The power simply underlies every atom. We either tap into it or we don't. We don't have to beg God to make the connection, to turn on the light. We don't have to wait ten days after putting in an application. We don't even have to make a deposit. We just have to relate.

WORSHIP is relating. It is admitting to the "hereness" and the "isness" of God. It is sensing his presence in all things. It is sinking into life knowing that underneath are the everlasting arms. It is finding strength for living not from some magically tapped reservoir outside of life but from the resources of God within life. The Incarnation, Christianity's unique testimony, says that here, clothed in humanity, is where it's at, where God is. Worship is the discovering of the divine in the commonplace. Worship is the ennobling of relationships.

And what a formalized rigamarole we have made of it! We have assumed that worship is some special arrangement of words. Always words! We say, "O come, let us worship," and having said it, think we have come and have worshiped. We say, "Praise the Lord!"—some of us more often than others—and assume that with the saying we have praised him, when all we have done is say, "Praise the Lord!" We are so busy running through the formulas, the supposedly potent phrases or exercises, that we often never get around to doing what we announce at the outset we are about to do: worship. For worship isn't crawling through a small hole into some theological wonderland. It is falling back upon God and finding that he is everywhere and anywhere you can fall.

NOT everyone talking about worship is doing it. In fact, when we're talking most about it, we're probably doing the least of it. It is like saying, "Be ye filled" to the hungry, and "Be ye clothed" to the naked, and neither filling nor clothing except with words. Strangely, when we do provide food and clothing and shelter and friendship and concern, we don't think of *that* as worship. Only talking seems to qualify as worship. And the more talking, the better. You have only to note how, outside a Quaker meetinghouse, Christians abhor silence, to realize how we equate sound and worship. One would think that silence were sinful and that worship must be orchestrated, verbal, full of sound. But worship is *relating*—in all the varied ways, in all the unexpected (as well as expected) ways that relationships come.

And we cannot relate to God without relating to people. Bringing a gift to the altar would seem to be an impeccable form of worship. But, says Jesus, if we find ourselves doing this while we have an imperfect relationship with our brother, we are to go out and perfect the relationship and then come back. One gets the feeling that if this kind of worship were taken seriously, the churches would be emptier than they are; we would all be out seeking reconciliation with someone! And would not the reconciliation be worship also? There is simply no way to get to God by shortcutting people. There is no such thing as worship in a cool, hygienic, placid vacuum. The place of worship is crowded with all the concerns that are man's—and God's.

Our view of worship is something like our view of prophecy, in which, again, we envision God pulling switches to sink this armada, rescue that expeditionary force, condemn that nation, prosper this one. God, pleased by his people humbling themselves, pushes the Dow-Jones up fourteen points—that's the picture, and it, too, is a demeaning one. God long since created the laws, physical and moral, of cause and effect. If we as a nation or as individuals pursue a certain course, certain things are going to happen, as surely as the planets revolve. The nation or individual that lives by violence will die by violence—this is the way things happen because it is the way people are built. The nation that debauches itself will inevitably lose the qualities that give it meaningful endurance.

THIS is not mystery, not whim; it is moral arithmetic. God doesn't have to shoot down targets, one by one. He has already called the shots. We are being continuously made and unmade by what we do, what we think, how we relate. The power to become is there, within us, around us, of the essence. Prophecy is not the ability to outguess God. The gift of prophecy is the gift of discerning, in the providence of God, the inescapable effects that specific causes will produce. A tower will stand as long as its center of gravity falls within its perimeter. The moment the center of gravity moves outside, the structure will collapse. That is as much the law of God as are the Ten Commandments, and vice versa. The same law that, broken, causes the tower to fall, obeyed, causes it to stand.

Come, let us worship *that* kind of God!

How Do I Know When My Prayer Is Answered?

THE ASSUMPTION is that if you get what you asked for, then your prayer was answered, and if you didn't, it wasn't. This doesn't take into account that so often when a prayer is "answered," we're less prone to credit God than when it was not answered. What we get, we tend to take for granted and as our due; what we don't get, we blame on God. Either way, we're preoccupied with what, from our point of view, looks like personal advantage.

More and more, I'm wondering if prayer has anything much at all to do with that sort of thing. Suppose one prays to find a ten-dollar bill lying on the sidewalk. For that ten-dollar bill to get there, someone has to lose it, assuming that no one is going around intentionally dropping ten-dollar bills. To pray, in effect, "God, please see to it that someone loses money so I can find it," is not an especially selfless prayer. Of course, we would not pray it quite that way. We would prefer that it all be very anonymous, no faces attached—a sort of high-level-bombing approach to prayer.

There is something else. In order for a prayer to be answered at a particular point, the machinery has to be put into motion long before the prayer is prayed. But if the answer is already in the pipeline, is it the prayer now that put it there then? Would it have come through anyway? Does it come because God is betting that you will pray and thus validate his answering? If the prayer is not forthcoming by a cutoff point, will the answer be stopped in its tracks, never to reach the intended recipient?

None of this is meant to downgrade prayer, but to upgrade it to the extraordinary, indispensable, priceless component of life that it really is. We simply cannot begin to understand prayer as long as we think of it as the price of material blessing, coin of the spiritual realm. I think we so often do not know when our prayer is answered because we are looking for the wrong evidence.

In the first place, if, many times, we got what we asked for, we would not achieve what we thought we were seeking but would be in a worse jam than ever. Someone has said, "The gods answer the prayers of those they wish to punish." I am glad now that I didn't get, through the years, some of the things I have prayed for. At some points I could have been too easily satisfied. In our prayers, we tend to be short-range askers. God, like any loving parent, tends to give long-range answers. A child does not necessarily get what he asks for. But did you ever stop to ponder how much of the satisfaction was not in the getting, anyway, but in the asking? Asking presupposes a special kind of relationship. There is trust and confidence in a childish request. The big thing is that there is somebody to ask, someone who cares.

So how do you know when your prayer is answered? The yearning intent of prayer is answered in the praying itself. The answer is in learning how to pray a prayer that is answerable. The life one is living ("prayer without ceasing") constantly feeds the pipeline from which some day, at a time of need and in recognizable form, will emerge answers one has been creating, with God. This much, at least, is up to us. What is beyond that much is up to him.

Let us pray.

111

"Then We Will Believe" — the Impossible Dream

TIME: What in retrospect we have come to call Good Friday of Holy Week, though to at least some of the onlookers it was Bad Friday of the unholiest week of their lives. *Place*: The hill of crucifixion. We move in on the central cross of three. *Characters* (for our purposes here): The chief priests, lawyers and elders, defenders of a faith they felt was being challenged, even blasphemed. They stand before the cross, shoring up religious preconceptions that allow them to stay comfortably dead. "Let him come down from the cross," they are saying, "and then we will believe him."

This is not the way belief was, is or ever shall be generated.

As a matter of fact, what they were trying to do—and what we so often try to do—was keep control of their believing, set their own rules for it. But when it comes to believing by faith, you simply do not set your own rules. You do not believe because you see. Rather, you see because you believe. You do not believe because you're front row center at a miracle. Rather, you are witness to and even participant in miracles because you do believe. They were turning the whole process of believing upside down, and of course nothing happened.

What they were looking for, and what we, their counterparts in and out of church, are so often looking for, was not a suffering savior but a Houdini.

"He saved others," they said, "but he cannot save himself."

Exactly!

For the instant an act of redemption becomes self-seeking and self-serving, it ceases to be redemptive. One saves others precisely because one does not save oneself. The cross—and the Christian life, to the extent that it takes its cues from the cross—is totally vulnerable. It is in

112

vulnerability that spiritual power lies. What we should be singing about is not the sentimentality of the cross but the vulnerability of the cross. It is in vulnerability that life's deepest meanings lie.

Let Jesus come down from the cross, and at that moment he is as bereft of inner resources as the rest of us. Furthermore, if we can get him down from his cross (or force him to show credentials we issue him), he is at our mercy, not we at his. For then we have made him jump when we say jump. And one of the troubles with miracles (as in other measurements such as attendance records, numbers of conversions, budget figures), he always has to jump higher the next time, for only an old miracle surpassed is a new miracle. Miracles, by our nature, have to escalate. We keep putting the bar higher and higher. We keep finding it harder and harder to take yes for an answer. And we think that if we say, "All right, then, I won't believe unless—" this gives us some hold on God.

But belief is not a boon we confer upon God. It is a boon he confers upon us. The unconquerable humility of the cross eloquently witnesses to religious know-it-alls of every generation that suffering, not security, is the stuff of redemption. And that if we demand a miracle as the price for believing, we will never believe.

Thanks for Nothing

WE ARE things-oriented, on our knees as well as on our toes. We ask God for things as if we were ordering from a mail order catalogue, and we give thanks for things as if we were signing a receipt for merchandise delivered. We measure with the senses, and things—unlike attitudes, emotions, motivations—are so eminently measurable. It is, for example, so much harder to measure a church than it is to measure a church building. It is so much harder to measure the thoughtful intention than the frequently awkward expression. It is so much easier to measure the few well-defined sins of the flesh than the multitude of not-so-easily-definable sins of the spirit, maybe in part because we are so regularly guilty of the latter. ("How great, O Lord, are the sins I have not committed!")

So our thanks once a year tend to be voiced in terms of turkey drumsticks, cranberry sauce, pumpkin pie and the like and at other times in the appropriate equivalents. We are thankful for the seeables and the tasteables, for the roof over us, for clothes and cars and bank accounts and salary checks. But when you stop to think about it, how demeaningly measurable becomes the amazing grace of God when reduced to timbers and calories and dollars! What do things, and even events, have to do with God's grace?

Recently I read the thrilling story of a wife's fearless rescue of her husband, caught in the cave-in of a well he was digging. By sheer pluck she managed to clear the debris from his face so that he could breathe. When help arrived and he was pulled free, she murmured as we all would be likely to do in such a situation, "God is good to us!" But would God's goodness have been less if her husband had died? Is God good to us when events work out as we hope they may, and less good when they do not? In life or in death, in fullness or in leanness, in health or in sickness, how could God be other than good? We ask even that much of a mutual guarantee in a wedding service!

There is something basic and irreducible about thanksgiving which does not relate to things but which rather relates to sheer joy of recognition. Prayer first of all and most of all exclaims happily, "God, it's you! You're here!" Prayer is the affirmation of a loving relationship. It is not the asking for what we think we do not have, but the knowing that we already have what is most important.

We have the broad sky that reaches all the way to some incomprehensible boundlessness. Talk about eternity! Look above you on a clear night and you can see forever

114

from where you stand. We have sunsets that dazzle the soul. We have air to breathe, polluted by our own wastes, to be sure, but literally the breath of life nevertheless, that we cannot store up within ourselves but on which we must depend one breath at a time. One of the most remarkable non-things for which to be profoundly thankful is the capacity to be aware of our own existence and to attach meaning to it. This is surely one of God's greatest gifts.

I wonder if, in fact, the non-possessables, the no-things, may not be the greatest gifts of all.

Come, let us give thanks!

Alibiing with the Bible

IT HAS OCCURRED to me that very often the Bible is used to alibi why we are not where we ought to be when we ought to be there. During the earlier days of civil rights, and even yet, Bible verses were freely and piously quoted as justification for violating the gospel. Slumlords, politicians and too often clergymen and church members thought they could run to the Bible and there take refuge from Christianity. Poor old Ham (he of the Shem and Japheth team), who suddenly became one of the best-thumbed characters of the Old Testament, was more welcome in print in uptight white homes and churches than I suspect he would have been in person.

One of the most reprehensible examples of alibiing is what so many otherwise decent and Bible-believing Christians have done with "the poor you have with you always," making it a biblical brush-off for any and all suggestions that the poor are not only a legitimate but a top-priority concern of the church. The context of the statement puts it in a totally different light, which is not surprising, since the poor were very much in the mind and heart of Jesus, as even his inaugural scripture reading in the Nazareth synagogue evidences.

You remember the incident. As it is told in Mark 14, it took place at the home of Simon, where a woman broke open a bottle of costly perfume and poured it over the head of Jesus. Whereupon, as the story goes, "Some of those present said to one another angrily, 'Why this waste? The perfume might have been sold for thirty pounds and the money given to the poor.' " The next words are dramatically descriptive of that time and of our time: "They turned upon her with fury." Can you imagine it? Yes, I guess you can, for you too have seen emotional violence when the poor become alibis. Jesus says, "Let her alone. Why must you make trouble for her? It is a fine thing she has done for me." Then comes the much-abused truth: "You have the poor among you always, and you can help them whenever you like; but you will not always have me."

In other words, some tasks and responsibilities and opportunities are of short duration, and some are never ending. That's far from the usual sniff, "Why help the poor? They will always be around, no matter what!"

It is revealing that although "the poor you have with you always" is often quoted as an excuse for not doing something, it is seldom or never quoted as a motivation for compassion, which it is. Our misuse is a biblical alibi if I ever heard one.

Jesus wrapped up the story beautifully. "She has done what lay in her power." We're power-conscious and power-hungry these days. I think that more lies in our power to do—about anything, including poverty—than we suspect. But it so often looks harder to do the things we can do than to do the things we can't do.

The Bible is no hiding place for those who would use it to subvert even God himself. Biblical alibiing is one thing we might give up, at least for Lent.

God Is Working. Of Course!

PERHAPS there is not that much importance to be attached to how we describe things, except that how we do it describes not only what we are talking about, but ourselves. Of late, I have been hearing and seeing the statement, "God is working. . . ." It's usually attached to a particular place: "God is working in Africa, or Indonesia, or America." Or it may be attached to certain categories of people: "God is working among youth, or Episcopalians, or Jesus People" or whatever.

The picture that this brings to my mind is of a God who has been stirred by our prayers or by a fortuitous circumstance into unusual action out of usual inaction. It is almost as if we think the world runs on its own momentum until and unless God happens to take an interest in what's on the agenda and drops in to give personal supervision.

This is not only an inadequate view of God, but it offers small encouragement to faithfulness by God's people. If nothing is going to happen anyway until God "works," then what's the use of our doing anything? For then we cannot be as sure of God as we are even of the deodorant whose users in the television commercial happily testify, "It's working!" any time and every time a deodorant is supposed to be working. We need to be reminded that God is working everywhere all the time, not just in some places some of the time. He is working when things don't seem to come off, and he is working when they do. He is working through Joseph's brothers as well as through Joseph.

I think that part of our problem is that word "working." It tends to superimpose God upon his creation, as if it had of itself the capacity to exist with or without him, or as if—and some Christians have no trouble believing this—it operates under some other management when God is not available, Satan being the most ambitious and currently publicized stand-in.

This raises for me the question of whether it is God's function and nature to "work" or whether it is his function and nature to "be." When I contemplate the tremendous and overriding fact of God's being, that he simply is, other things, including my own responsibilities, begin to fall into line. He is there in every experience, even those we cannot understand. He is there in every faithfulness, in every sorrow, in every joy, in every success, in every defeat. We could not have any experience if he were not there. His being is the ground of our being. In him we live and move. He is creation and he is presence and he is power. Our fulfillment as believers does not result from seeing things work out as we presume they should—even when sometimes that happens—but from being faithful in Christ's name to his commandments to love and to share. Faithfulness does not require "success" as the measure of its worth. As love is its own measure, so is faithfulness.

Granted, there are times in history when certain things can and do happen and other times when they cannot and do not. The times are in God's hands. But we need to remember that all times are in his hands and not just some of them. It is of more than passing interest that when God identified himself to Moses, he did not present a job description. He said the most important thing about himself that could be said: "*I am.*" That is the most exciting, the most awe-inspiring, the most utterly reassuring fact that we too can know about God. He is!

Wanted: More Than a Cuddly Savior

THERE IS something lovable, terribly human and transcendently divine about a baby. When one looks into unblinking, direct infant eyes, they are full of eternity. It is easy to fall down and worship at a cradle. Perhaps that is why Christmas is so widely observed, even by those who make no religious response to it. It is a kind of Birthday of Babyhood. We sing, "The little Lord Jesus lay down his sweet head." We like little and sweet things at Christmas. We are intrigued by a cuddly Savior.

It is very hard for Christians to let the little Lord Jesus out of his crèche. As long as he is safely contained in a manger, he is silent and helpless—"trailing clouds of glory," maybe, but no lightning or thunder.

Alas! Babies do not stay babies and cuddly Saviors do not stay cuddly. They learn to talk. They grow up. They grow out of our control. They burst from their cradles to stride the world. They learn to love. They learn to die. No parent actually wants his child to stay young, and the poignant way to describe retardation is to speak of the little one who never grew up. But it is nevertheless very hard for parents and Christians to free their little ones and ever to admit that they have become big ones.

Jesus faced such reluctance in his own time. When he went back to teach in his hometown synagogue, his neighbors, astonished by his wisdom and his works, voiced a question that neighbors often ask about the grown-up local youngsters. "Is not this the carpenter's son?" They obviously couldn't imagine how anybody they had known from childhood could possibly amount to anything—which may be at the root of some of our own problems. How do you take seriously anyone whose nose you have wiped? I daresay that if a former schoolteacher of the President of the United States should come to the White House for a visit, as she sat across from him at his desk, she would see not a world leader but a little boy holding up his hand to ask permission to go to the bathroom. "I've known *him* all his life!" is the put-down that is the greater judgment upon self than subject. A prophet is without honor on his own street mainly because everyone else on the street is without honor. An absent or visiting messiah always seems to be the authentic one—perhaps the reason why so many of us do not take ours seriously. We have known him since his babyhood in creches all over the country. We tried to keep him under our Christmas trees, and when that failed, we said, "Is not this the babe of the manger? How peacefully he slept! Little Lord Jesus, no crying he made."

There is a time for a baby and there is a time for a man. There is a time for Christmas and there is a time for Calvary. There is a time for wonder and there is a time for commitment. Perhaps Christmas is not a day that should last all year. Perhaps it has lasted too long already. Perhaps, if we would let the babe grow up, we would grow, too. We talk of putting Christ back into Christmas. Perhaps the greater need is to put Christmas ahead into Christ.

For the incarnation is not a drama of a nestling, containable, cuddly Christ, but of a Christ at large in the world who demands my faith, my life, my all. For the Christmas moment, yes, all is calm. But wait and watch all heaven break loose!

Unless I See the Print of the Nails, I Will Not Believe

IS THE CHURCH what it says it is? Is the Christian who he says he is? Where are the nailprints? They are the proof. This statement of Thomas' that always seemed to me to be brash and arrogant, becomes, when it is turned upon us, a demand that is not only legitimate and proper but inescapable. And I get the feeling that I am seeing, and displaying, very few nailprints these days.

The compulsion for painful accreditation has taken some weird turns. Whole sects have been developed around various kinds of self-mutilation. There were—and are—the flagellants, for example, who scourge themselves in public penance. You can see photos in the papers during the Easter season of a procession of priests carrying a man-sized cross along the Via Dolorosa in Jerusalem, a feat which presumably would give the bearer at least a few blisters, though nobody is being crucified. In front of a cathedral in Mexico City I have seen men and women "walking" on their knees across the vast courtyard to the church doors. There is this compulsion to feel pain, to have evidence that can be looked at, checked out.

We do it in our own symbolic ways, from sighing heavily in public at the state of the world, to attending church meetings that we don't especially enjoy, to putting up church buildings, to basking in religious hostility, to—well, whatever your own brand of sophisticated flagellation happens to be. We have this feeling that we've got to do something, and we don't know quite what to do, or we're not prepared to do what we sense we ought to do. So we do whatever we think looks good both to ourselves and to others.

Now, church building, meeting-going and such are not necessarily bad. Our mistake has been that we assumed they were necessarily good. They are bad if they are places to hide and good when they are tools for the building of something else.

Hiding places never seem to get very scuffed up; tools that are used always do. There are church members who are so fearful of the new carpet's becoming threadbare, or of a scratch on the paint, that they regard people—children and young people especially—as a hazard. Where are the scars in our churches? Where are the prints of the nails, or even the marks of the Scotch tape? The Thomases are not asking for destructiveness but for evidence that Christians regard people as being more important than things.

The trouble is that you can't set out to *be* sacrificial. Plotting the route, doing it by calculation, kills the whole thing. A sacrifice has to be, for the sacrificer, comparatively spontaneous and unrehearsed. As soon as he says, "Hey, man, I've got a pretty good set of nail prints going here!" they cease to be convincing. For one thing, you never know what the market for "nailprints" is going to turn out to be, or what will qualify as nailprints. For another, when you're in the process of earning them, you would avoid the experience if you could. The getting has no grandeur in it. There is only something in you that says, "This I must do, if I am to live with myself." No guarantees of anything except integrity. No assurance that it will work out to your personal advantage or even to God's glory. No risk-free, 90-day trial offer. But the resulting scars, or lack of them, will forever after say something about the real self, the authentic you, when at some unexpected place at some unanticipated time the challenge is directed at your church or mine, or at you or me, "Unless I see the print of the nails, I will not believe." Could it be that we believers are the reason there are so many unbelievers?

Take My Life and Let It Be

THERE is a certain amount of confusion about punctuation. A classic story one of my English teachers told eons ago was about how students should punctuate the sentence, *Mary a pretty girl was walking down the street.* One youngster, sly beyond his years, said, "I'd make a dash after Mary." Actually, he then would have had to make a dash after "pretty girl" too, but that would probably have been all right with him.

It is in poetry, especially, that punctuation problems often show up, and therefore, in hymns and hymnbooks, for hymns are poems. So it was that on a recent Sunday, I saw staring up at me the hymn title, "Take My Life and Let It Be." This was in a hymnbook in which the title is the first line of the hymn, and that was assuredly the first line of this one. But there is no comma at the end and so, when you're singing this hymn, you aren't supposed to stop or even pause wistfully but to keep going before you even take a breath. It's supposed to come out, "Take my life and let it be consecrated, Lord, to thee."

Poetic form and limited lung capacity here produce odd

bed fellows. For when God takes you up on the proffer of your life, he's not going to let it just sit there. He's going to shake it considerably, and in ways you can't contemplate or predict. The happy surprise is that shaking up is not that unpleasant for the shaken person who is committed to something. It is the bystanders, the outsiders, the non-involved, the spectators, who are the tongue cluckers and the headshakers.

For what is order to the committed, is disorder to the uncommitted. What is rightside up to the one who gives himself, is upside down to the fellow who never got the hang of selflessness. When Paul and Silas arrived in Thessalonica, some of the townspeople complained, "These men who have turned the world upside down have come here also." The complainers didn't know which end was up. And when the madman who lived among the tombs and pigs was healed, the locals got uptight when they found him clothed and in his right mind. They had grown comfortable with his wrong mind. For them, wrong was right.

Well, the problem is not so much where you put your comma when you sing, as where you put it in your whole approach to living. "Take my life and let it be" is the impossible petition of a man or woman who wants the best of two worlds but who doesn't want to pay the list price for either. It is the plea of the fearful person who thinks to play it safe—standing with one foot in the rowboat and one on the dock while the gap widens.

History is made by those who give themselves to something, wholly, sacrificially, singlemindedly. Those who will be remembered save their comma till they get past the consecration. They are the fortunate ones for whom life suddenly becomes livable, believable, meaningful.

Perhaps it's just that we have been brought up on the idea that "it is a terrible thing to fall into the hands of the living God." Into whose hands would you rather fall? As David put it, when he was up against hard options: "Let us fall now into the hand of the Lord; for his mercies are great."

My Will Be Done

IT IS so close to what our intent is so much of the time, that the altered word may not even be noticed. I don't know of anyone who out loud substitutes "My" for "Thy" in the Lord's Prayer, but I strongly suspect that this is very often an under-the-counter petition. In prayers of our own composition, we tend to be more forthright about it. If we do manage to gulp, "Thy will be done," we regard ourselves with pleased awe, as if we had just performed a massive act of courage.

But what in the world is courageous or sacrificial about asking God—Mind and Order of the universe, Love itself!—to do his will through us and our ambitions? Are we *afraid* of what he may do? Do we suppose that he intends, given a foot in the door, to make things unendurable for us, to pour it on, wear us down, take delight in our discomfort? Come on, now! If we can't trust God's love for us and his concern for our best interests, what is left to trust? What is the point of the Apostles' Creed, the Bible, the particular doctrines of your church, the church itself, if you are fearful of entrusting yourself to God's hands?

I think there is more here than meets the ear. I suspect that we are reluctant to say, "Thy will be done," not because we don't know what we would be letting ourselves in for, but because we do know. We, in fact, know more about God's will than we are ready to admit to knowing. Does anyone suppose, for example, that racial justice—or any other kind of justice—is *not* God's will? Do you have to ask if it's God's will that you speak a kind word, that you feel the hurts of the world? Whatever reconciles, whatever beautifies, whatever heals, whatever comforts, whatever companions—this has *got* to be God's will.

Which is not to say that God hopes to run you ragged. In fact, I get a little weary with the run-ragged school of theology, and with churches that attach the "God's will" label to anything and everything that happens under the sponsorship of the congregation. A profusion of church meetings can be as jealously self-centered as any individual's preoccupation.

If you don't happen already to have a pretty good idea of what is God's will in a given situation, praying "Thy will be done" is not a secret password that automatically relieves you of choices. You still have decisions of your own to make.

Sometimes we are prepared to seek God's will only regarding those matters we don't much care about one way or the other. Or regarding those that are the "spiritual" decisions, as opposed to any which deeply affect "real life." We try our wants on for sighs and let God have first crack at those in which we have no passionate (most of the time financial) interest. The chances are that he is no more interested in them than we. So before "thy will" can mean very much, "my will" must mean a great deal.

It seems to me that if we think of prayer not as a channel of getting but as a channel of growing, other things begin to fall into place. Including whose will you honestly have in mind.

All Things Work Together

I WAS BROUGHT UP on Romans 8:28. It pulled my mother and father through the Depression, through illness, through surprises, disappointments, sorrows and joys. Many times it was unclear to me how things could be working together for good. Especially "to them that love God." Those who loved him seemed in fact often to wind up with the short end of the stick.

It is still one of the most meaningful passages of the Bible for me. But I no longer see it as a passive, whatever-will-be-will-be kind of concept. I see it as a dynamic initiative, a resource of Spirit. For in the innocent by-stander incidents of life, the distinctive of faith as against un-faith is not so much what happens as it is what one makes of what happens. The fact is that for everyone all things work together. The difference is whether things—all things—work together for good or for ill. Though the happenings, the abilities, the resources, the "things" may be almost identical for two people, one may be destroyed by them and the other strengthened. It's not the things that are different but the working together of the things.

And they don't work together all by themselves while you sit there watching. It is not the automatic and passive submission to whatever comes as being the will of God that is the secret of buoyance, but that God helps us make the best of it instead of the worst of it. It is not what happens to us that is determinative but what happens in us. Have you noticed that when we pray, we tend to pray about the outside instead of the inside? We pray about the things that confront us instead of about the attitudes by which we confront things.

I am thinking here of my personal spiritual life, not of methods for dealing with the lives of other people. I find faith and encouragement in telling myself to make the best of it, but I find only arrogance and insensitivity in my telling someone else to make the best of it. Jesus, to my knowledge, never urged anyone, "Keep a stiff upper lip!" He never said—though some people think it is divine revelation—"Grin and bear it." He did in many ways make the point that the remedies for our ills lie often within our own attitudes; that joy does not spring from joylessness; that peace is not a product of guilt; that health does not come from fear. So it may be altogether unconvincing and even unchristian to tell someone else, "All things are working together for your good." Especially if you are speaking from a comfortable room to someone with no home, or with a turkey drumstick in one hand to someone who is hungry. But it is very useful to tell it to *yourself* when your hopes have fallen in or when you have suffered unmerited harm or when someone is deliberately abusive.

I like the way the Living Bible puts my favorite verse: "We know that all that happens to us is working for our good if we love God and are fitting into his plans."

So the question is not, "Is it?" The question is, "Are we?"